Eberly Library
Waynesburg College

Waynesburg, Pennsylvania

Presented by
Rea Andrew Redd

QUANTRILL AND HIS
CIVIL WAR GUERRILLAS

BY THE SAME AUTHOR

The Complete and Authentic Life of Jesse James
Badmen of the Frontier Days

QUANTRILL
and his
Civil War
Guerrillas

by

CARL W. BREIHAN

PROMONTORY PRESS

NEW YORK CITY

Published by Promontory Press, a division of A & W Promotional Book Corporation, 95 Madison Avenue, New York, N.Y. 10016, by arrangement with The Swallow Press, Inc., 1139 S. Wabash Avenue, Chicago, Ill. 60605.

Library of Congress Catalog Card No.: 73-79822
ISBN: 0-88394-002-7

Copyright © 1959 by Carl W. Breihan.
All rights reserved.

Manufactured in the United States of America.

DEDICATION

To My Children
Carol Ann, Carl Jr., and Janis Sue

Oh, the dread of those wild days!
A fearful tale they tell,
When rang the woodlands' echoes 'round
To warlike scream and yell;
When fiercely met the hostile bands
And deadly grew the strife,
And wildly, with the clash of arms,
Went up the shrieks for life.

Acknowledgment

Grassroot research comes under the heading of hard labor, and it would have been nearly impossible to complete this work without the gracious assistance of many friends and old-timers.

Some of these fine old gentlemen have crossed the Great Divide to their just rewards, yet I thank them in the names of those who remain of their families. In this category falls Harry Younger Hall, nephew of Cole Younger, Jesse Edwards James, son of Jesse James, Charles Kemper, that grand old fellow of Independence, Missouri, and Bill Stigers, who resided at St. Joseph, Missouri, and whose mother was named after Quantrill.

I also appreciate the editorial assistance of Glenn Clairmonte and the continued encouragement of Uncle Charlie E. Bell of Louisville, Kentucky, thorough student of the Old West, A. Maxwell of Lexington, Missouri, and Ed Bartholomew, a fellow writer and traveler on old trails.

There are many others who deserve a vote of thanks: the many historical societies, the various state archives, and many writers' organizations. And to any and all who have been so kind in the struggle to compile this book I express heartfelt thanks and gratitude.

CARL W. BREIHAN

Contents

Prelude to the Civil War	11
The Quantrill Family	17
Quantrill in Kansas	25
The Black Flag	41
Quantrill at Richmond	47
Character Studies	52
The Palmyra Butchery	61
Battles of Carthage and Wilson's Creek	75
Battle of Lexington	80
A Narrow Escape	97
Blue Cut Again	103
Independence and Lone Jack	109
The Sacking of Lawrence	116
After Lawrence	135
Bloody Bill Anderson	145
The Battle of Centralia	151
Deaths of Todd and Anderson	158
The Last of Quantrill	162
Roster of Guerrillas	166

Illustrations

John Brown	33
General Jo Shelby	34
General Jo Shelby's wife	34
Quantrill at Lawrence, Kansas	35
Quantrill, 1862	36
Jesse James, 1863	37
Jesse James, 1870	37
Frank James at an early age	38
Frank James	38
Frank James, 1898	39
Fletch Taylor, Frank James, Jesse James, 1866	39
Captain Bill Anderson	40
Captain George Todd	40
Affidavit concerning Cole Younger gun	88
James Younger	89
Coleman Younger	89
Newspaper clipping regarding Mrs. Caroline Quantrill	89
General James H. Lane	90
Sam Hildebrand	90
Colonel Upton S. Hays	91
Captain John Jerrette	91
Captain William H. Gregg	91
Lee McMurtry and William Hulse	91
Quantrill's watch	92

John Brown's Colt	92
Guns of Jesse James, Frank James, and Cole Younger	93
Captain Wagner's tombstone	93
Captain George Todd's grave	93
Monument to Quantrill raid victims	94
Cole Younger gun	94
Massachusetts Street, Lawrence, 1863	95
Ruins of Lawrence	96

Prelude to the Civil War

The Territory of Kansas had not yet been admitted to statehood when John Brown came into prominence there as an abolitionist and agitator. During this era every territory not yet organized into a state became a field of conflict: should it be a state of free citizens, or should the slave system prevail?

John Brown was one of the most colorful and controversial figures of his time: a man of strong convictions, deeply religious, fanatical in his zeal to free the slaves. He led a group of rugged men on raid after raid to punish slaveholders. On the night of May 24, 1856, not long after an outrageous attack by pro-slavery fighters on Lawrence, Kansas, he conducted the massacre of five of his opponents at Pottawatomie Creek.

Ossawatomie, Brown's home, was burned in August of that same year by those who hated him, and his son was killed. Sympathizers in Massachusetts, the state of his birth, collected funds to supply him with rifles, and he pondered long on how to use them most effectively. At last he conceived the daring idea of establishing a stronghold in the mountains of Virginia as a refuge for runaway slaves. This secret plan culminated on the night of October 16, 1859, when he led a band of his followers into Harper's Ferry and seized the national arsenal.

That action was at the time said to be a signal for a general insurrection of slaves; but Colonel Robert E. Lee, later commander of the Confederate forces, suppressed the raid, and John Brown was captured. His audacious act proved disastrous to his men, as well, and resulted in further embittering the South. The incident at Harper's Ferry turned out to be a prelude to the Civil War.

Colonel Lee reported:

I have the honor to report for the information of the Secretary of War, that on arriving here on the night of the 17th, in obedience to Special Orders No. 194 of that date from your office, I learned that a party of insurgents, about 11 P.M. on the 16th, had seized the watchmen stationed at the armory, the arsenal, the rifle factory, and bridge across the Potomac, and had taken possession of these points. They then dispatched six men under one of their party, called Captain Aaron C. Stevens, to arrest the principal citizens in the neighborhood, and incite the negroes to join in the insurrection. The party took Col. L. W. Washington from his bed about 1:30 A.M., and placed arms in the hands of the negroes. Upon their return here, John E. Cook, one of the party sent to Col. Washington's wagon, two of his servants, and three of Mr. Allstadt's for arms, ammunition, etc.

As day advanced, and the citizens of Harper's Ferry commenced their usual avocations, they were separately captured, to the number of forty, as well as I could learn, and confined in one room of the fire-engine house of the armory, which seems early to have selected same as a point of defense. About 11 A.M. the volunteer companies from Virginia began to arrive, and the Jefferson Guards and volunteers from Charleston under Captain J. W. Rowen, I understand were first on the ground. The Hamtramck Guards, Captain V. M. Butler; the Shepherdstown troops, Captain Jacob Reinhart; and Captain Alburtis' company from Martinsburg arrived in the afternoon. These companies, under the direction of Colonels Taylor and Gibson, forced the insurgents to abandon their positions at the bridge and in the village, and to withdraw within the armory enclosure, where they fortified themselves in the fire-engine room and house, and carried ten of their prisoners for the purpose of insuring their own safety and facilitating their escape, whom they termed hostages. . . .

After sunset more troops arrived. Captain B. B. Washington's company from Winchester, and three companies from Fredericktown, Maryland, under Col. Shriver. Later in the evening the companies from Baltimore, under General Charles Edgerton, Second Light Brigade, and a detachment of marines commanded by Lieut. J. Green accompanied by Major Russell of that corps, reached Sandy Hook, about one and a half miles east of Harper's Ferry. At this point I came up with these last named troops, and leaving Gen. Edgerton and his command on the Maryland side of the river for the night, caused the marines to proceed to Harper's Ferry and placed them within the armory grounds to prevent the possibility of the escape of the insurgents. Having taken measures to halt in Baltimore, the artillery companies ordered from Fort Monroe, I made preparations to attack the insurgents at daylight. But for the fear of sacrificing the lives of some of the gentlemen held by them as prisoners in a midnight assault, I should have ordered the attack at once.

Their safety was the subject of painful consideration; and to prevent, if possible, jeopardizing their lives, I determined to summon the insurgents to surrender. As soon after daylight as the arrangements were made, Lieut. Stuart, First Cavalry, who had accompanied me from Washington as staff officer, was dispatched under a flag, with a written summons . . . Knowing the character of the leader of the insurgents, I did not expect it would be accepted. I had therefore directed that the volunteer troops, under their respective commanders, should be paraded on the lines assigned them outside the armory, and had prepared a storming party of twelve marines under their commander, Lieut. Green, and had placed them close to the engine-house and secure from its fire. Three marines were furnished with sledgehammers to break in the doors, and the men were instructed how to distinguish our citizens from the insurgents; to attack with the bayonet, and not to injure the blacks detained in custody unless they resisted. Lieut. Stuart was also directed not to receive from the insurgents any counter propositions. If they accepted the terms offered, they must immediately deliver up their arms and release their prisoners. If they did not, he must, on leaving the engine-house, give me the signal. My object was, with the view of saving our citizens, to have as short an interval as possible between the summons and the attack.

The summons, as I anticipated, was rejected. At the concerted signal the storming party moved quickly to the door and commenced the attack. The fire-engine within the house had been placed by the besieged, close to the doors. The doors were fastened by ropes, the spring of which prevented their being broken by the blows of the hammers. The men were therefore ordered to drop the hammers and with a portion of the reserve, to use as a battering-ram a heavy ladder with which they dashed in a part of the door and gave admittance to the storming party. The fire of the insurgents, up to this time, had been harmless. At the threshold one marine fell mortally wounded. The rest led by Lieut. Green and Major Russell, quickly ended the contest. The insurgents that resisted were cut down by bayonets, and their leader, John Brown, by the sword of Lieut. Green. Our citizens were protected by both officers and men, and the whole was over in a few minutes.

From the information derived from papers found upon the persons and among the baggage of the insurgents, and the statements of those now in custody, it appears that the party consisted of nineteen men, fourteen white and five black. That they were headed by John Brown, of some notoriety in Kansas, who in June last, located himself in Maryland, and at the Kennedy farm, where he has been engaged in preparing to capture the United States works at Harper's Ferry. He avows that his object was the liberation of the slaves of Virginia, and of the whole South; and he acknowledges that he has been disappointed in his expectations of aid from the black as well as the white population, both in the Southern and the Northern states. The blacks whom he forced from their homes in this neighborhood, as far as I could learn, gave him no voluntary assistance . . . The result proves that the plan was the attempt of a fanatic or madman, which could only end in failure; and its temporary success was owing to the panic and confusion he succeeded in creating by magnifying his numbers.

In his address to the court on November 2, 1859, John Brown said:

I have, may it please the Court, a few words to say. In the first place, I deny everything but what I have all along admitted, the design on my part to free the slaves. I intended to have made a clean thing of that matter, as I did last winter when I went into Missouri and there took slaves without the snapping of a gun on either side, moved them through the country, and finally left them in Canada. I designed to have done the same thing again, on a larger scale. That was all I intended. I never did intend murder, or treason, or the destruction of property, or to excite or incite slaves to rebellion, or to make insurrection.

I have another objection; and that is, it is unjust that I should suffer a penalty. Had I interfered in the matter which I admit, and which I admit has been falsely proved, for I admire the truthfulness and candor of the greater portion of the witnesses who have testified in this case—had I so interfered in behalf of the rich, the powerful, the intelligent, the so-called great, or in behalf of any of their friends, either father, mother, brother, sister, wife, or children, or any of that class, and suffered and sacrificed what I have in this interference, it would have been all right; and every man in this court would have deemed it an act worthy of reward rather than punishment.

This court acknowledges, as I suppose, the validity of the law of God. I see a Book kissed here which I suppose to be the Bible, or at least the New Testament. That book teaches me that all things whatsoever I would that men should do to me, I should do even so to them. It teaches me, further to "remember them that are in bonds, as bound with them." I endeavored to act up to that instruction. I say, I am yet too young to understand that God is any respecter of persons. I believe that to have interfered as I have done—as I have always freely admitted I have done—in behalf of His despised poor, was not wrong, but right. Now, if it is deemed necessary that I should forfeit my life for the furtherance of the ends of justice, and mingle my blood further with the blood of my children and with the blood of millions in this slave country whose rights are disregarded by wicked, cruel, and unjust enactments, I submit. So let it be done! . . .

In any event, it is known that it was John Brown who started the border wars which continued until Federal troops suppressed the combatants. On November 2nd he was sentenced to be hanged on December 2nd. On the morning of his execution he handed his jailer a brief note which later proved to be a true prophecy:

I, John Brown, am now quite certain that the crimes of this guilty land will never be purged away except with blood. I had thought, and still believe, that without very much bloodshed it might have been done.

John Brown was led to the gallows and there, in sight of

the beautiful country he had hoped to gain by treason and uprising, he paid the extreme penalty of the law. He met death bravely and with the firmness and unbatting eye of a hero.

The South called him a fanatic; the newspapers of the Northern states pictured him having the exalted courage of a martyr. People in the South believed that the raid on Harper's Ferry and Brown's execution would open the eyes of the entire population to the crime and madness of abolition concepts. The Northern view was to the contrary. The manifestations of sympathy for John Brown were widespread; in many cities and towns in the Northern states and territories the church bells tolled on the day of his hanging. His body was taken to North Elba, New York State, where many of the New England clergy extolled his virtues and his devotion to the cause of freedom.

The Quantrill Family

A man who was to make his career in the border conflict between Missouri and Kansas was William Clarke Quantrill. From the start he was mean and vicious, and his boyhood pranks were merely the forerunners of the crimes he perpetrated when he became a man. Despite this, the legend long persisted among Southerners that he wore a halo of righteousness.

Cruelty was a part of Quantrill's nature. When a young boy he liked to catch two cats, tie their tails together and hang them over a wire fence or clothesline, and watch them claw and fight frantically until both were dead. He took the family cow of one of his neighbors and painted the unfortunate animal red. Since the paint could not be removed in time, the cow died. He hated school and, when compelled to attend, made life miserable for the teacher.

Once he took a young girl to the church belfry and locked her in the tower all night, while the whole town searched, her parents frantic with terror and grief. When the child was finally found she was suffering from shock and exposure, on the verge of collapse. Yet young Quantrill thought it was a good joke.

Small wonder that his mother sent the incorrigible boy to Illinois with the Clapp family. She said she hoped that a change of scene might improve him. In the town of Mendota young Will Quantrill was restless and homesick. He wrote home that he needed money and asked his mother to send his books and a few other of his belongings so that he could sell them and buy things he needed. She sent them, but he was unable to sell them. Discouraged, and feeling that he had been cast off by his family, he stopped writing home.

His mother did not hear from him again until February, 1856, when he was teaching school in Fort Wayne, Indiana. He did not, of course, tell his mother that he had left Illinois under a cloud. Later it was learned that there had been a killing in Mendota and that young Quantrill had been arrested on suspicion. When apprehended he told the authorities that while working in a lumber yard he had been attacked by a robber one night and in self-defense had shot the man. Since no witness appeared against him, he was released and advised to leave town.

Whatever had actually happened in the lumber yard, Quantrill was now changed. The following spring he did return to Canal Dover, Ohio, where his mother lived. But restlessness struck him again, and when he next left Ohio he failed to pay his board bill in the Ulrichsville school district. His harassed mother had appealed to Mrs. H. V. Beeson, who had experienced many a difficulty with her husband Henry, to take the wayward son with him to Kansas. As the boy headed westward he was moving into a destiny dark and infamous, one which was to make his name a word used to frighten naughty children.

To comprehend the character of this strange individual, it is necessary to look into the history of his family. Upon arriving in America prior to 1812, the Quantrills first settled in Hagerstown, Maryland. Though the name has a French ring, the Christian names of the early members of the family give the impression they were of English stock: William, Thomas, Jesse, Archibald. And Will Quantrill's grandfather, Captain Thomas Quantrill, claimed that his ancestors had come from England.

This Captain Quantrill was an outstanding personality who attracted attention wherever he went. Six feet tall and very respectable-looking, he was the Hagerstown blacksmith after having successfully served as an Army officer. He married Miss Judith Heiser, sister of William Heiser, who was for many years president of the Hagerstown bank. One of the sons of this union was Thomas Henry (called Henry), the father of the boy who was to become the dreaded outlaw. Others of his

THE QUANTRILL FAMILY

children were Archibald Rollin Quantrill and Jesse Duncan Quantrill.

To be sure, the family was not without notoriety even in those early days, for one of the sons—it is not now possible to establish which one—became a pirate on the high seas. He operated for many years on the Gulf of Mexico, between Galveston Island and the mouth of the Sabine River.

Captain Thomas Quantrill often visited his son Henry in Canal Dover (now Dover), Ohio, where Henry was regarded as a handsome man of fine personality. The Captain, by the time he had become a portly old gentleman, moved to Washington, D. C., and died there suddenly, of apoplexy.

Henry's brother Jesse was sent to school in New York City, but he failed to apply himself to his studies, and after returning home he got into a little trouble. Since this son was the Captain's favorite, he had always been indulged and allowed to grow up in idleness. A dashing young fellow with certain unconventional instincts, he nevertheless married Miss Mary Lane, daughter of Seth Lane, one of the foremost Hagerstown citizens. Mary was heir to a large sum of money which was not to be touched until she reached her majority. However, through trickery Jesse managed to withdraw the money from the bank and squandered it. Later he had the audacity to try to collect the sum a second time when his wife came of age, claiming that the bank had had no legal right to relinquish it earlier and had thus violated Seth Lane's trust.

Jesse moved to Williamsport, Pennsylvania, where he engaged in the grocery business and failed. Not a bit discouraged, he went back to New York City and, representing himself as the son of a certain well-known wealthy Virginia merchant, he bought on credit a large stock of goods which he ordered shipped to Baltimore. The merchant discovered the swindle in time to stop part of the consignment, but the crafty Jesse had managed to dispose of the rest of the merchandise in a way which baffled all attempts to trace it. He next tried bankruptcy, but his application was denied when it was proved to be based on fraud, and he was sent to prison. Oddly enough, for six months his beautiful wife, the former Mary Lane, shared his prison cell. He finally secured release on the ground of conspiracy by the merchant from whom he had stolen the goods.

While in prison Jesse studied law under the direction of William Price, one of the leading lawyers in Maryland, whose interest in this Quantrill was no doubt the result of influence on the part of Jesse's in-laws. After his release Jesse went to St. Louis, Missouri, where again his criminal tendencies soon got him into trouble with the law. His faithful wife secured his release this time, and they boarded a boat for Cincinnati, Ohio. Before the boat had docked his considered use of a pen was the cause of his next predicament, for the forgery was quickly discovered; but once again he escaped punishment.

From Cincinnati Jesse moved to New Orleans, where he led a dissipated life and neglected and abused his wife. She fell seriously ill, and, strange as it may seem, her condition appeared to work a change for the better in Jesse. They returned to Cincinnati. There, as the consequence of another forgery, he was thrown into prison. Mary bailed him out, and he repaid her loyalty by deserting her and fleeing town. The next time she heard of him he was in Hagerstown, again in trouble over forgery. He escaped conviction, went to Philadelphia, committed forgery again, was tried, convicted, and sentenced to three years in prison.

Mary Lane Quantrill finally divorced Jesse and remarried. Her second husband was Andrew Cowton, the proprietor of the United States Hotel at Cumberland, Maryland. In the meantime Jesse drew a second sentence, this time of seven years, but he was free again in 1848.

Mrs. Cowton was in her apartment at the United States Hotel when the man she had divorced was suddenly ushered in by a servant. He dismissed the servant, bolted the door, and declared he had come to kill Mary. When she screamed for help he caught her by the throat, threw her to the floor, and cocked a loaded revolver in her face. Miraculously the gun missed fire, and the infuriated man was drawing a wicked-looking

THE QUANTRILL FAMILY

knife when several persons burst into the room and rescued the frightened young woman. Jesse was arrested, found guilty of assault with intent to kill, and sentenced to a long term.

Jesse must have possessed a fascinating personality, for he won the confidence of the prison officials and was allowed considerable freedom, even acting as trusty to guard over the other prisoners. In 1851 he was pardoned on condition that he leave the state and never return. After a year or two spent as a jockey and horse dealer in Canal Dover, Ohio, where his brother Henry lived, he disappeared. However, news of his escapades reached that village periodically for many years afterward. Under various aliases (such as Doctor Hayne) he married and deserted six women.

Jesse's brother Archibald was a printer who at one time worked as a compositor on the *National Intelligencer* at Washington, D. C. He must have been one of the younger sons of Captain Thomas Quantrill, for it was in 1862 that he married a Mary Sands whose age was given as thirty-two. She was a staunch supporter of the Union. Her brother, George Sands, was United States Collector of Internal Revenue under President Lincoln. When General "Stonewall" Jackson and his Confederate troops passed through Frederick, Maryland, this Mrs. Archibald Quantrill and her daughter Virginia stood at their gate and defiantly waved the Stars and Stripes in the faces of the Confederates. A soldier cut the flag from Mrs. Quantrill's hand with his sword. General Jackson rebuked the soldier and, turning to Mrs. Quantrill, raised his hat, saying, "To you, madam, not to your flag."

The poet Whittier may have immortalized the wrong woman, for the one he mentioned, Barbara Frietchie, was a bedridden lady.

Henry, that son of Captain Thomas Quantrill who was the father of the notorious guerrilla, was somewhat above the average in education, and he also was addicted to sharp practices. In Canal Dover he confiscated some of the school funds entrusted to his care and used them to publish a Lightning Calculator. He also published a number of books on mathematics by means of school funds. This misuse of the money was discovered by the school board and brought to the attention of the public.

Henry Quantrill vowed he would kill the man responsible for this bad publicity, and late one evening he entered the home of H. V. Beeson with a cocked revolver in his hand and murder in his heart. Beeson grabbed an iron poker and struck Henry Quantrill over the head with it, knocking him unconscious and incidentally saving his own life. Neighbors rushed in and carried the beaten man out of the house and to his home.

About the same time Henry was having some trouble with a Mrs. Roscoe, the vivacious wife of a Frenchman and a teacher of painting. Henry was reported to have made some derogatory remarks about her character, so when she met him on the street she gave him a public lashing with a bullwhip, much to the delight of the townsfolk.

Despite his reputation, in 1849 when the Canal Dover Union School was organized, Henry Quantrill was appointed assistant to the principal. In 1851 he became the principal and continued in this office until his death of consumption in 1854.

The Quantrill family Bible records the birth date of William Clarke Quantrill as July 31, 1837, and this record together with other data was published in the Louisville (Kentucky) *Courier-Journal* of May 13, 1888, to refute the outlaw's one-time claim that he had become a guerrilla to avenge the death of his elder brother at the hands of Kansas "Redlegs" during the Kansas-Missouri border warfare.

MARRIAGES
Thomas Henry Quantrill and
Caroline Cornelia Clarke—October 11, 1836

BIRTHS
William Clarke Quantrill, July 31, 1837
Mary Quantrill, September 24, 1838
Franklin Quantrill, November 12, 1840
MacLindley Quantrill, December 18, 1841

Cornelia Lisette Quantrill, June 20, 1843
Thompson Quantrill, October 3, 1844
Clarke Quantrill, September 5, 1847
Archibald Rollin Quantrill, September 27, 1850

DEATHS

MacLindley Quantrill, died August 26, 1842
Cornelia Quantrill, July 28, 1844
Clarke Quantrill, September 5, 1847
Archibald Quantrill, March 2, 1851.

At the time these records appeared in the paper, Mrs. Thomas Henry Quantrill, formerly Miss Caroline Clarke, showed visitors the old family Bible and said, "We had eight children in all, but four of them died in infancy. Here in the old Bible in which the family records were kept you see the names and dates. These records were all made by my husband. I have never written a line in this Bible since his death, which accounts for the balance not being in. Only one of my children is still living—Thompson, who lives in Montana, where he has a family and is doing well. My daughter Mary died in 1865. She was never married. My son Franklin died six years ago, leaving his wife and four daughters, two of whom are grown. One is a teacher at Canal Dover."

Quantrill's mother had been born in Somerset County, Pennsylvania, but her family soon moved to Chambersburg, where her parents died when she was only about six months old. She was taken into the home of an uncle, Alexander Thompson, who was judge in Somerset and Bedford Counties. Caroline was raised to be a good homemaker and cook, and in fact she was always a devoted wife and mother. While rearing her large family she had to stay closely at home, and in time she was known never to visit the neighbors or go to church. It may be that Quantrill's inclination to be a "lone wolf" stemmed from his mother's side; from his father who was very sociable he must have inherited some of his other characteristics.

Mary Quantrill was a cripple and was seldom seen outside the home, and this may have been the main reason her mother remained at home so constantly. Mary passed away at the age of twenty-five, in 1863, at about the time her infamous brother was at the zenith of his wild career in Missouri.

The many intelligent people in the Southland who persist in depicting Quantrill as a brave and misunderstood commander must be ignorant of the facts, for there is nothing in the documents to warrant their admiration. As a matter of fact and record, Quantrill never rode with all his men on any raid except one—for the pillage of Lawrence, Kansas, he was accompanied by about three hundred men. At all other times he sent out a small detachment of from twenty to thirty (occasionally as many as fifty) under the command of his lieutenants who owed him no actual allegiance.

These petty leaders, who by no means considered themselves Quantrill's subordinates, included Bloody Bill Anderson, George Todd, Bill Gregg, Fletch Taylor, John Thrailkill, John Jarrette, George Shepherd, Cole Younger, Kit Dalton, John Hildebrand, Arch Clements, and occasionally Frank James, brother of the notorious Jesse James. Appended to this work is a list of the nearly three hundred men who were at one time or another known to have ridden with Quantrill on his murderous missions.

It was Quantrill's custom to pillage then put to the torch small undefended towns or villages, deliberately murdering any who dared to protest. Now and then, such as in Boonville, Missouri, both Northerners and men in favor of the South banded together in defense against such raids, the Southerners stipulating only that they should not be asked to fire on regular Confederate troops. Several times a town was saved from depredations by the guerrillas only by such concerted action.

Quantrill in Kansas

For a while after young Will Quantrill went to Kansas with Beeson nothing more was heard about him. At Independence, Missouri, Beeson purchased two ox teams and a wagon in which to make the rest of the trip through the very rough country. With Quantrill he headed for the area of the Marais du Cygne in Franklin County, Kansas, near Stanton, which is in Miami County. On March 22, 1857, they reached their destination.

Everywhere Quantrill heard rumors about a monster named Hamilton, an inhuman fiend who a year earlier had appeared in Linn County, Kansas, at the head of a hundred bloodthirsty men. He wantonly killed and looted, burned homes and fields of grain, and mercilessly persecuted everyone with anti-slavery sympathies. Capturing twenty of the most prominent citizens of Linn County, he bound them hand and foot and took them to a lonely spot called Trading Post on the Marais du Cygne River. Here he tied them to stakes and shot every one of them. Several of the victims were not mortally wounded, but they feigned death and later were able to tell the bloody story. John Greenleaf Whittier recorded it in these words:

Le Marais du Cygne

A blush as of roses
 Where roses never grew,
Great drops on the bunch-grass,
 But not of the dew!
A taint on the sweet air
 For wild bees to shun—
A stain that shall never
 Bleach out in the sun!

> Back, steed of the prairies,
>   Sweet songbird, fly back!
> Wheel hither, bald vulture!
>   Gray wolf, call thy pack!
> The foul human vultures
>   Have feasted and fled;
> The wolves of the Border
>   Have crept from the dead. . . .
>
> On the lintels of Kansas
>   That blood shall not dry!
> Henceforth the Bad Angel
>   Shall harmless go by;
> Henceforth to the sunset,
>   Unchecked on her way,
> Shall Liberty follow
>   The march of the day!

Will Quantrill was intrigued by this desperate tale. When he arrived in Kansas in 1857, he was not quite twenty years old and boyish in appearance. He was decidedly blond, with fair skin and hair a pale yellow; it did not take on its reddish tint until years later. He was slim and well formed, but there was an indefinable something about him—perhaps the shifty eyes or the cruel mouth, which caused people to dislike him at first sight. There was something stealthy in his walk, his sidewise glance, his cynical, sneering attitude. True, he had an alert mind, but he was hard to get along with. He brooded over imagined insults and suspected any kindness shown him. He bore malice, cherishing it, waiting until he could wreak his venom. He was coldly calculating and had the patience to wait silently for the right time for his vengeance. Though mentally far above the average, his spiteful, belligerent nature turned his thoughts to bad instead of to good. He reasoned rapidly, and once his mind was made up he never changed it, perhaps because his clear logic covered all phases of any problem on which he concentrated.

He was never popular among men of his own age, being given to making abrupt and strange remarks. For instance, when strolling along the bank of the Marais du Cygne one day he pointed to a large branch of a tree extending horizontally over the road and remarked, "I could hang six men on that limb!" The conversation had been light and pleasant until that moment. People stayed aloof from such an odd personality, and young ladies were warned by their parents not to be seen in his company.

Consequently it was natural for Quantrill to find himself, in the wild new territory, surrounded by rough, tough men, many of them criminals. They were the ruthless, remorseless fruits of the warfare which existed between Kansas and Missouri over the slavery question. In less vicious circumstances Quantrill might have been considered a most disagreeable neighbor when he vented his malice by maiming a horse or poisoning some cattle. But it was hardly recognized that, under what he called strong provocation, he would shoot an adversary from ambush or knife him in the dark of night.

Quantrill's laziness, his propensity for taking life easy and letting others do the work, kept him from acquiring property as he would have liked to do. He had even wearied of teaching school. Restraint of any kind he would not tolerate. On those few occasions when he was working for other men, he was insubordinate, always wanting to take matters into his own hands. He freely admitted to his acquaintances that he wanted to arrive at fortune by some great stroke of luck. Certainly he had no intention of holding himself to any standard of honesty.

Quantrill cannot be placed in the category of the "badmen" of the Old West, such as Wild Bill Hickok, John Wesley Hardin, or even Billy the Kid. He was not an adventurer but was instead probably the all-time champion of murder. He did not personally kill his hundreds of victims, but he was responsible, inasmuch as they were ruthlessly massacred at his direct orders.

Both Beeson and a Mr. Torrey were from Canal Dover, and both were trying to befriend Quantrill for his mother's sake. It was their intention to take up land and farm. Most of the territory was held by squatters, who often sold their plots to the highest bidder. Beeson bought the squatter rights to a quarter section of good prairie land in Franklin County, and Torrey bought a similar right to land adjoining. Torrey also managed to buy a claim for young Quantrill, or Bill as he was now called, because, being under age, he could not legally acquire land for himself. Torrey paid $250 for a claim and held it for Bill, agreeing to pay Bill $60 for bidding it in at land sales and assigning the certificate to Torrey.

This claim had an old log cabin on it, and Beeson and his son Richard, Mr. Torrey, and Bill Quantrill all made their home there. In one corner of the only room there was a built-in bed in which the two men slept, while the two boys, Dick and Bill, rolled up in blankets on the floor in front of the fireplace. The Kansas nights were cold and, when the fire died down toward morning, the cabin reached the freezing point. Bill would roll himself in both blankets and leave young Beeson to shiver on the bare floor. The remonstrance of the men made little or no effect on Bill, who angrily resented their interference.

Colonel Torrey had a Mexican dagger with a long, keen blade, which he kept in his trunk as a souvenir of the Mexican War. One night Beeson awoke and saw young Quantrill standing over him, the dagger in his upraised hand, ready to plunge it into his heart. Beeson yelled and so surprised the young Bill that he halted, and that gave Torrey time to leap out of bed and disarm him. Beeson grabbed a stout hickory stick and lashed Quantrill until he begged for mercy.

"Bill," panted Beeson, "I hated to give you such a thrashing, but I hope it will make you think. Your good mother would be terribly grieved if she knew of your bad conduct out here. She confided in me that she hoped your coming out here would make a man of you. But it seems to me you are in league with the devil himself. I am sorry for the day I first laid eyes on you."

Bill sneered that for his part he was sorry he had ever laid eyes on Beeson and declared he was leaving. "I'm glad to be rid of you and your damned orders. On my own I'll be able to get somewhere."

Quantrill put a little distance between himself and the stick in Beeson's hand before he added, "You can go straight to hell, all of you! And let me tell you something before I go: you'll hear a-plenty about me before I pass off this no-good earth!"

How true that prediction was!

Quantrill prowled around the vicinity, and he often complained to people that Torrey and Beeson were cheating him. One John Bennington, a strong pro-slavery advocate, really believed that the two men were trying to cheat the boy out of his land. Emboldened by his talk with Bennington, Quantrill went to Torrey and demanded an additional ninety dollars for the claim he was holding. Of course Torrey did not want the matter brought into court, since his having assigned a piece of land to a minor was irregular, to say the least, so he agreed to pay him sixty-three dollars extra, in several installments. He was a little slow in making settlement because money was hard to get. Quantrill, urged on by Bennington, stole a yoke of oxen, five blankets, and two revolvers from Torrey.

A few days later, Beeson met Quantrill on the trail and told him that if he wanted to keep out of court he had better divulge the whereabouts of the animals. As a means of persuasion Beeson covered the younger man with a revolver, so Quantrill led him into a dense thicket, where the oxen stood still yoked together and tied to a tree. They had been neither fed nor watered and were so weak that they could hardly stand.

"Bill Quantrill," Beeson raged, "you're even worse than I thought. Mark my words! You'll come to no good end!"

The latter part of 1858 Beeson returned to Ohio to get his family, and several other Canal Dover families followed them to Kansas. Among them were some former schoolmates of Bill's—John Diehl, Charles Wood, George Hildt, and Alexander McCartney—who settled on adjoining claims in Johnson County. They named their place after an Ohio settlement, Tuscarosa Lake. Seemingly eager to be among old friends, Quantrill, then of legal age, also went to Johnson County, took up a claim, and settled among them.

The young men from Ohio sometimes gathered at Beeson's place on Sundays, but Quantrill usually spent that day with John Bennington, for Bennington fed his vanity. One Sunday the boys told Beeson they had to chase Bill out of the settlement for stealing. All winter they had been missing blankets, tools, and other things, and finally they had caught Quantrill in the act of plundering one of their cabins.

Quantrill could do nothing about his loss of standing, so he took the alias of "Charley Hart" and left Kansas. At first he went to Utah with a provision train for the soldiers who had been ordered there to quell the Mormons. In the "wild and woolly West" he was in his element. As Charley Hart he soon became expert at poker, faro, and blackjack. He was considered a very lucky dealer and player, though he may have been dealing from the bottom of the deck all the time. He was smart enough to cover his tracks during this period, with the result that not much information is available concerning it. Presently, however, he became involved in some trouble with the army officials in Utah and was requested to leave—perhaps because of his gambling operations.

Most of the writers on Quantrill to date have been taken in by the rumor he invented that his older brother had been murdered by Lane's Kansas Redlegs. He said he had joined his brother in Kansas, that they were on their way to California when a band of Jayhawkers in the command of Captain Pickens raided their camp, killed the older boy, and left him (Charley Hart) for dead, carrying off their valuables. He went on to say that friendly Indians came to his rescue, that later he joined Pickens' company where nobody recognized him, that of the thirty-two soldiers responsible for the death of his "brother" only two escaped his vengeance—and they got away by fleeing to California. (He may actually have known a Charley Hart about whom this was partially true.)

Another version of the story, equally false, which most of the writers on the subject of Quantrill in Kansas repeat, is that all the men he killed were shot squarely between the eyes. Yes, sir! right smack between the eyes!

The villainous Quantrill was merely creating fiction, portraying himself as an invincible hero. By a sort of self-hypnotism he believed himself justified in starting on a nefarious career of murder and plunder. Recent research has definitely debunked this myth.

Kansas in those years immediately preceding the Civil War was ripped by internal dispute and border warfare. Intense political hatred existed along the Missouri-Kansas border. Missouri, a slave state, wanted Kansas admitted to the Union as a slave state, too. Abolitionists in Kansas were determined to keep Kansas free and were leaders in founding the Underground Railroad, an immigrant aid society to help smuggle escaped slaves out of the South. Under its auspices, a great many easterners were brought to Kansas and Missouri to assist in the activity. Raids between the two states were frequent and from this tense, interstate conflict grew bands of "Redlegs"— freebooters who used the slave situation as an excuse to plunder and kill for personal gain. For every raid there was retaliation, and the Redlegs escaped any reprisal. Always on the move, they agitated the situation, which grew worse by the day.

The situation was made to order for Quantrill. Completely incapable of taking orders, it was natural that he should eventually organize a band of his own. But Quantrill's mind needed an excuse. He found it in his overactive imagination. It was typical of Quantrill that he chose to vent his anger against the State of Kansas in developing his amazing fiction. After all, it was Kansas who had thrown him out. In Quantrill's mind, the humiliation of being told to leave the squatters' town several years before resulted in his hatred of the entire State of Kansas. It gradually grew in importance in his mind until it became all-consuming. In the years that followed, Quantrill finally purged his entire distorted viewpoint by directing his homicidal viciousness against Kansas. But first he needed a reason. This was the lie that his brother had been murdered by Kansans—a lie which eventually became real in his mind.

Quantrill organized a band of men who believed they were rallying in defense of their home state against the depredations of Kansans under General Jim Lane. However, the rumbling of the heavy guns which forced Fort Sumter to surrender had hardly cleared before Quantrill was telling his men they were going to fight for the Confederacy. This choice gave Quantrill the lever he needed to prey openly upon Kansas—to murder, to maim, to plunder.

A graphic example of the terrible conditions existing along the Missouri-Kansas border just prior to the Civil War is the case of Russell Hinds. In the fall of 1860 a slave ran away from his owner and stopped at the home of John Turner near Pleasanton, Kansas. The Negro felt that he would find sanctuary among the Kansans who favored the Free-State Movement. Turner advised the slave to return to his Missouri owner, but the man refused to do so. Finally with the help of Russell Hinds, a friend, Turner was able to persuade the slave to return to his master near Pleasant Hill, Missouri. The master offered to pay Turner and Hinds the customary $25.00 reward for the return of a slave; but the men refused to accept it. Hinds, however, did accept a $5.00 expense reimbursement.

Several days later Hinds was arrested and charged with manstealing and carrying the slave back to Missouri for sake of the reward. The prisoner was tried before Judge James Hanway and found guilty by a jury of twelve men. On November 12, 1860, Russell Hinds was hanged on Mine Creek, in the timber, near the Missouri line. Turner escaped only because Hinds did not implicate him in the incident. Hinds lost his life for accepting $5.00 expense money.

John Brown

Rare photo of General Jo Shelby's wife, never before published.

General Joseph Orville (Jo) Shelby, noted Confederate cavalry leader and active in Missouri during the Civil War.

Photo taken at Lawrence, Kansas, by M. A. Kennedy. This is the only photo of Quantrill while he was using the name of Charley Hart.

Quantrill, 1862. Taken at Independence, Missouri, by Mr. Burdge.

Jesse James in 1870.

Jesse James, 1863.

Frank James at an early age. *Bartholomew Collection.*

Rare photo of Frank James, never before published.

Left to right: Fletch Taylor, Frank James, Jesse James, in Nashville, 1866.

Bartholomew Collection.

Captain George Todd. Photo never before published.

Captain Bill Anderson.

The Black Flag

Major John Neumann Edwards, adjutant to Brigadier General Joseph O. Shelby, after the war became editor of the Sedalia (Missouri) *Democrat*. In one of his articles he had this to say about William Clarke Quantrill:

One half of the country believes Quantrill to have been a highway robber crossed upon a tiger; the other half that he was the gallant defender of his native South; one half believes him to have been an avenging nemesis of the right; the other a forbidding monster of assassination. History cannot hesitate over him, however, nor abandon him to the imagination of romancers. He was a living, breathing, aggressive, all-powerful reality, riding through the midnight, laying ambuscades by lonely roadsides, catching marching columns by the throat, breaking it upon the flanks and tearing a suddenly surprised rear to pieces; vigilant, merciless, a terror by day and a superhuman if not a supernatural thing when there was upon the earth blackness and darkness.

Of course, Canal Dover, Ohio, Quantrill's original home, could not be considered the South. And as for his being a gallant defender, Quantrill never defended anything except himself, claiming allegiance to the Confederacy only because that suited his purpose.

Major Edwards further said, of the men who formed the Quantrill band:

As strange as it may seem, the perilous fascination of fighting under a black flag—where the wounded could have neither surgeon nor hospital, and where all that remained to the prisoners was the absolute certainty of speedy death—attracted a number of young men born of higher destinies, capable of sustained exertion in any scheme or enterprise, and fit for callings high up in the scale of science or philosophy. Others came who had deadly wrongs to avenge, and they gave to all their combats that sanguinary hue which yet remains a part of the guerrilla's legacy.

Almost from the first, a large majority of Quantrill's original command had over them the shadow of some terrible crime. This one recalled a father murdered; that one a brother waylaid and shot; another his house pillaged and burned while at peace at home; this one a robbery of all his earthly possessions; this one driven away from his own like a thief in the night; this one threatened with death for opinion's sake; this one proscribed at the instance of some designing neighbor; this one arrested wantonly and forced to do the degrading work of a menial; while all had more or less of wrath laid up against the day when they were to meet, face to face and hand to hand, those whom they had good cause to regard as the living embodiment of unnumbered wrongs.

Honorable soldiers in the Confederate Army—amenable to every generous impulse and exact in the performance of every manly duty —deserted even the ranks they had adorned, and became desperate guerrillas because the home they left had been given to the flames, or a gray-haired father shot upon his own hearthstone. They wished to avoid the uncertainty of regular battle and know by actual results how many died as a propitiation or a sacrifice. Every other passion became subordinate to that of revenge.

Millions of men and boys, through the years since that deplorable period of American history, have read of the black flag and the black oath which Quantrill's guerrillas were required to take when enlisting in that outlaw band. It seems to be true that such an oath was administered, at least in the early days of the group and, in view of Quantrill's nature, it matches his other acts. According to J. Frank Dalton, the old ex-Quantrillian who passed away in 1951, the oath was introduced by these words:

The purpose of war is to kill! God himself has made it honorable, in the defense of principles, for did He not cast Lucifer out of Heaven, and relegate rebellious angels to the shades of hell? The love of life cannot be measured, under two conditions: One is when our surroundings are happy and our attachments numerous; the other is when our liberties are subjugated, peace destroyed, and everything we hold dear torn from us, until we realize that contentment, love, hope, have forever vanished. We fight that the former happy condition may be regained, and we fight because the latter condition leaves us no other occupation.

You have voluntarily signified a desire to cast your fortunes with us. By so doing, remember that our purpose is to tear down, lay waste, despoil and kill our enemies. Mercy belongs to sycophants and emasculated soldiers. It is no part of a fighter's outfit. To us it is but a vision repugnant to our obligations and our practices. We recognize but one power to separate us in the hour of peril, and to succor one another at all hazards we have pledged ourselves more sacredly, and are bound by ties much stronger than honor can impose. With this understanding of what will be required of you, are you willing to proceed?

The candidate having assented, the following oath was administered, being repeated by the candidate as the initiating officer spoke it slowly, sentence by sentence:

In the name of God and Devil, one to punish, the other to reward, and by the powers of light and darkness, good and evil, here under the black arch of heaven's avenging symbol, I pledge and consecrate my heart, my brain, my body, and my limbs, and I swear by all the powers of hell and heaven to devote my life to obedience to my superiors; that no danger or peril shall deter me from executing their orders; that I will exert every possible means in my power for the extermination of Federals, Jayhawkers and their abettors; that in fighting those whose serpent trail has winnowed the fair fields and possessions of our allies and sympathizers, I will show no mercy, but strike with an avenging arm, so long as breath remains.

I further pledge my heart, my brain, my body, and my limbs, never to betray a comrade; that I will submit to all the tortures cunning mankind can conflict, and suffer the most horrible death, rather than reveal a single secret of this organization, or a single word of this, my oath.

I further pledge my heart, my brain, my body, and my limbs, never to forsake a comrade when there is hope, even at the risk of great peril, of saving him from falling into the hands of our enemies; that I will sustain Quantrill's guerrillas with my might and defend them with my blood, and if need be, die for them. In every extremity I will never withhold my aid, nor abandon the cause with which I now cast my fortunes, my honor, and my life. Before violating a single clause or implied pledge of this obligation, I will pray an avenging God and an unmerciful devil to tear out my heart and roast it over flames of sulphur; that my head may be split open and my brains scattered over the earth; that my body be ripped up and my bowels torn out and fed to carrion birds; that each of my limbs be broken with stones and then cut off by inches, that they may be fed to the foulest birds of the air; and lastly, may my soul be given into torment that it may be submerged in melted metal and be stiffened by the fumes of hell, and may this punishment be meted out to me through all eternity, in the name of God and the Devil. Amen.

Dalton said that Quantrill demanded this black oath of his men during the early stage of the war but dispensed with it later when there was less time for dramatics.

Of the black flag itself, perhaps some Missouri woman actually did make one, but it was probably not used extensively. At least, research has not revealed verification of the story that there was one—and yet the rumor about Miss Annie Fickle is worth considering. In the latter part of 1861 this charming woman let it be known that she wanted to have a talk with the famous guerrilla leader. Quantrill agreed to meet her near the little church in Sni-A-Bar Township. Quickly coming to the purpose of the interview, Miss Fickle showed him the proclamation of Colonel (later Brigadier General) Asa P. Blunt, threatening execution for all guerrillas captured. Then she praised Quantrill and his men, "the faithful Southerners throughout the State of Missouri," and ended with a slogan:

> And ever let your battle cry be
> "Quantrill and Southern supremacy!"

The climax of this tête-à-tête came when Annie Fickle unfolded a large piece of quilted alpaca, three by five feet in size, with QUANTRELL in bright-colored letters stitched in the center of it. "Quantrill's Black Flag" was tacked to an eight-

THE BLACK FLAG

foot pole, and it may never have been cairried as an official banner, though perhaps it was unfurled on special occasions. Certainly it was never used after the sacking of Lawrence, for Frank James and Cole Younger both stated they had never seen it. J. Frank Dalton and Allen Parmer also said there had never been such a flag. Yet Kit Dalton, another of the old original guerrillas, wrote a book entitled *Under the Black Flag* after interviewing J. Frank Dalton.

The guerrillas established their headquarters in the rugged area of the Sni Hills lying south of the Missouri River below Kansas City and Westport, Missouri. Through this region of timbered hills, deep ravines, and high bluffs, flowed the Sni and the Blue Rivers, as well as numerous other streams. The location certainly was ideal for a hideout: hills with rocky ledges covered with vegetation so dense that a bird could hardly fly through it.

In this fastness the outlaws unobserved made their preparations for raids and battles. They could rush forth and, after committing their villainy, could dash back to cover; and once they had ridden into the uncharted forest they were practically beyond pursuit. No one dared to follow into that wild terrain of ambush and treachery. And so, night after night, Quantrill and his gang sallied forth, trusting to the sympathies of the surrounding population, and there rarely was any danger that they would be intercepted or challenged. Many people openly showed sympathy for the Union but in secret aided the cause of the South, and vice versa. By the time the Federal authorities learned of this, it was too late for them to counteract the hit-and-run attacks of the guerrillas.

In 1860 Quantrill had returned to Kansas from Utah, still under the alias of Charley Hart, and he boarded at the Whitney home on the bank of the river. Perhaps the reason he used the name Charley Hart was that too many of the crimes committed under his real name were known. At the time of the sacking of Lawrence, he gave orders to spare the Whitney house because he had been well treated there.

Shortly after his return, Quantrill became involved in a number of shady deals, associating himself with characters whom the police were watching; and "Charley Hart," too, soon had the police on his trail. After one scrape he escaped into Missouri and for some months lay low just across the border from Miami County, Kansas. He persuaded four devil-may-care young fellows to join him in robbing the home of a wealthy slaveholder named Morgan Walker, who lived in Jackson County, about ten miles from Independence, Missouri. "Hart" then betrayed his associates to the intended victim, and three of them were shot and killed, Hart himself killing one of them.

However, on his return to Miami County, Kansas, he was locked up in the Paola jail. Missouri friends, who had no knowledge of the various charges against him, bailed him out, and he quickly joined them beyond the jurisdiction of the Kansas officials. Prior to this he had publicly sympathized with the Kansas Free-State movement; now he went over to his Missouri comrades and became the leader of that state's most daring pro-slavery guerrillas. The most successful raids of the Missouri marauders were under his leadership.

Quantrill at Richmond

Regarding Quantrill's boast that he held a colonel's commission in the Southern forces, it is at least true that in certain instances the Confederate War Department allowed commissions, to be later confirmed by the authorities at Richmond. However, there is no record in the captured Confederate files that such a commission was ever awarded William Clarke Quantrill.

It is known that in the fall of 1861 Quantrill took a trip to Richmond accompanied by two of his men, Andy Blunt and Charley Higbee, and that, to his surprise and chagrin, the authorities rejected his plan for a general massacre and the hoisting of the Black Flag by the Confederacy. A fair field and honorable battle did not suit Quantrill, for he preferred the tactics of ambush, plunder, and slaughter. Nevertheless, during his conference with the Secretary of War he asked to be commissioned as a colonel under the Partisan Ranger Act. General Louis T. Wigfall, formerly a Senator from Texas, was present and reported that Quantrill asked for recognition by the Department so as to have accorded him whatever protection the Confederate Government might be able to exercise. He stated that he would have the required complement of men in one month after returning to western Missouri.

"The border warfare is desperate," Quantrill explained to the Confederate officials, "but everything in the service is desperate and requires desperate measures. To succeed, the Confederacy must put up an unceasing and desperate fight."

Secretary of War James A. Seddon responded, "Of course, war has its amenities and refinements, but in the nineteenth century it is plain barbarism to talk of a 'black flag.'"

"Barbarism!" cried Quantrill, his steel-blue eyes flashing with anger. His entire manner changed, his whole attitude underwent a transformation. He hotly declared, "Barbarism, Mr. Secretary, means war! And war means barbarism! Since you have touched upon this subject, let us discuss it a little. Time has its crimes as well as its men. For twenty years this cloud has been gathering. For twenty years, inch by inch and little by little, those people called Abolitionists have been on the track of slavery. For twenty years the people of the South have been robbed—here a Negro, there a Negro. For twenty years hates have been engendered and wrathful things laid up against the day of wrath. This dark cloud now has burst—do not condemn the thunderbolt!"

The Confederate Secretary of War bowed his head.

Quantrill got up and walked over to him, saying, "Who are these people you call Confederates? Unless they succeed, they will be rebels and outcasts, traitors, food for hemp and gunpowder. There were no great statesmen in the South, or this war would have broken out ten years ago, perhaps before that! Today the odds are desperate. The world hates slavery, the South is fighting the world. The ocean belongs to the Union Navy. There is a recruiting officer in every port in foreign countries. I have captured and killed many who did not know the English tongue. Mile by mile the cordon is being drawn about the granaries of the South. Missouri will go first, next Kentucky, then Tennessee, and by and by Mississippi and Arkansas—then what? Must we put gloves on our hands and honey in our mouths to fight this war as Christ fought the wickedness of the world?"

The Secretary of War did not speak; it was evident that Quantrill did not wish him to do so.

"You ask the impossible thing, Mr. Secretary," Quantrill went on. "This secession or revolution, whatever you choose to call it, cannot conquer without violence, nor can those who hate it and hope to stifle it resist without vindictiveness. Every struggle has its philosophy, but this is not the hour for philosophy or philosophers. Your young Confederacy wants victory. It wants champions who are not judges. Men must be killed. To impel the people to passion there must be some slight illusion mingled with the truth; to arouse our people to enthusiasm, something out of nature must occur. That illusion should be a crusade in the name of conquest, and the something out of nature should be the Black Flag! Woe be unto all of us if the Federals come with an oath of loyalty in one hand and a torch in the other!

"I have seen Missouri bound hand and foot by this Christless thing called conservatism, and where today she should have two hundred thousand heroes fighting for liberty, beneath her banners there are scarcely twenty thousand."

"What would you do, Quantrill, had you the power and were given the opportunity?" the Secretary of War inquired.

"Do?" snapped Quantrill. "Do? Why, I would wage such a war, and have such a war waged by land and sea, as to make our surrender forever impossible! I would cover the armies of the Confederacy all over with blood! I would invade, I would break up foreign enlistments by indiscriminate massacre, and I would win the independence of my people, or I would find them their graves!"

"And our prisoners? What of them?"

"Nothing of them, Mr. Secretary. There would be no prisoners. Do they take prisoners of my men? No! Surrounded, I do not surrender; surprised, I do not give way to panic; outnumbered, I rely upon common sense and stubborn fighting. Proscribed, I answer proclamation with proclamation; outlawed, I feel through it with my power; hunted, I hunt the hunters in turn. Hated and made blacker than a dozen devils, I add to my hoofs the swiftness of the horse and to my horns the terrors of a savage following. Kansas should be laid waste at once! Meet the torch with the torch, Mr. Secretary! Meet pillage with pillage, slaughter with slaughter, subjugation with extermination. Now, you have my ideas of war, Mr. Secretary, and I'm sorry they are not in accord with yours, nor with the ideas of the Government you have the honor to represent."

Surely Quantrill here displayed the gift of oratory. He was ambitious. Through his distorted vision he considered himself worthy of promotions and honors. He believed he had earned adulation and distinction, and he was never averse to saying so. But in Richmond he discovered, much to his disgust, that the men in power did not think as he did; that the Confederacy was not depending on his exploits in Missouri. He was not wined and dined in Richmond as he had confidently expected to be; on the contrary, he was even denied a colonel's commission. He pined to be honored as a hero, and he was hurt and humiliated at the outcome of this visit.

But, without the commission he coveted, he bowed himself away from the presence of the Secretary of War, and in resentment left the capital city of the doomed Confederacy. He traveled through Mississippi, and while in that state he stopped several days at the camp of some Missouri troops on Black River, about twelve miles east of Vicksburg.

When he returned to Missouri and walked into the camp of his followers, he was very much depressed. His discouragement was augmented at sight of the pathetic remnant of his gang. Still, General Sterling Price promised him great things, insisting there was plenty of time for promotions. (Price had himself fared but little better at the hands of the Richmond officials; as a matter of record, Confederate President Jefferson Davis held General Price in open contempt.)

Since Quantrill was not willing to bow to authority, Generals Jo Shelby, Sterling Price, and Ben McCulloch were all on his hate list. He considered all three of them inefficient and unworthy of their rank. Never once did he act under direct orders from Richmond; all his actions were according to decisions made by himself or his band. However, at times he fought alongside regular Confederate troops under Shelby and his Iron Brigade, under Price, or under McCulloch (who was later killed at the Battle of Pea Ridge, Arkansas, by the noted sharpshooter Wild Bill Hickok). But Quantrill never fought with any of them for any length of time. He preferred ambushing and harassing the Union troops, with his guerrillas divided into small bands.

But Quantrill continued to hope for a commission. At any

rate, he enlisted under General Price, who may very well have given him a temporary field commission; at least it was never confirmed at Richmond. And it does not seem logical that Quantrill ever held the rank of colonel, in view of the fact that a colonel's appropriate command is a regiment. Quantrill never at any time commanded more than one hundred of his own men, and most of the time the number was less than seventy-five. Of course, during the raid on Lawrence more than three hundred participated on his side, but Confederate Colonel Joseph Holt rode along that day. Even if Quantrill had been a colonel he would have been subordinate to Holt, a regular, while Quantrill even with a field commission would have had no authority over regular Confederate troops. Technically, during what is called Quantrill's raid on Lawrence he would have been only second in command if he had been operating as an army man.

Quantrill never was given an opportunity to show if he had any "military genius." In his peculiar kind of warfare he was somewhat of a wizard in maneuvering his men to take advantage of any shortcomings of his opponents. Whether he could have successfully handled a brigade or a division will never be known. Let us not forget that even in handling a small body of men he had very able assistants, such as Cole Younger, George Todd, and Bloody Bill Anderson.

Character Studies

Certain writers have given William Clarke Quantrill the glowing title of The Blond Apollo of the Prairies. While in his youth he was considered handsome, he was hardly a Greek god in any sense. Not only was he vicious but he did not have any justification for being so. Several members of his organization had reason to wreak vengeance, but the guerrilla chieftain merely indulged his desire to destroy. Even though he had been born a Northerner he did not side with the Unionists—perhaps, as he claimed, because he hated Kansas after he inspired the Kansans to drive him out of the state. He chose to fight for the Confederacy because it was a chance to hit back at the people of Kansas. His declarations at Richmond and his later actions were proof enough of his underlying motive.

Cole Younger, whose full name was Thomas Coleman Younger, was one of the first men to join Quantrill's group and one of the first to leave it. To those who knew Cole it was clear that he had suffered terrible wrongs and endured many provocations before he became a guerrilla, for he was never a bloodthirsty or merciless man. He was a dead shot, an expert with firearms, and it was said of him that he never missed a target. Only on one occasion did he commit an inexcusable act, and that was when he killed several Redlegs with a captured Federal Enfield rifle. It is inconceivable that he would have conducted such an experiment against regular Union soldiers. He was brave to the point of recklessness, desperate to rashness, and even courageous in showing mercy. For instance, during the massacre at Lawrence he secretly saved the lives of several old men, despite Quantrill's strict orders that not one male citizen should be spared.

After the close of the Civil War there were many people

who credited their lives to Cole Younger, who had prevented their ruthless killing while they were prisoners of Quantrill's gang. His many acts of kindness stood him in good stead when he himself was a prisoner in the Minnesota State Penitentiary—sentenced to life imprisonment for his part in the abortive raid on the Northfield (Minnesota) bank in 1876 with Jesse James. Many remembered his courage on the battlefield and came to his aid. Not only people without influence but some with powerful connections worked until they eventually secured his release, after twenty-five years.

Cole's family long bore the brunt of persecution. Thomas Coleman Younger, commonly known as Cole, was born January 15, 1844, on the Younger farm near Big Creek at Lee's Summit, Missouri. There Cole learned the art of handling firearms and soon became an expert. It had been his father's wish that he do so, for Cole often assisted him with the mail route, where dangers were ever present. Colonel Younger operated several United States mail routes for the government many years. One of the routes was between Harrisonville and Butler, with Cole carrying the mail on this route when he was but seventeen years old.

In ante-bellum days Colonel Younger represented Jackson County three times in the Legislature, and was also Judge of the County Court. He was a wealthy man and was the prey of the Kansas Jayhawkers who raided constantly into Missouri and along the Kansas border. It was a desperate fight between those who wanted Kansas admitted as a Free State and those who wanted her admitted as a Slave State.

As those turbulent days brought the Civil War closer and closer, Colonel Younger relinquished his post as Judge of the Jackson County Court and moved his family to his farm at Harrisonville, Missouri.

The clash between the North and the South became more and more inevitable, and adherents of the North formed themselves into military companies. One of these companies, called Neugent's Regiment of the Enrolled Missouri Militia, was stationed near the county seat at Harrisonville.

Captain Irvin Walley, in command of a company of Neugent's Militia, hated Cole Younger because the young man refused to encourage his sister to favor the captain. To make matters worse, Colonel Mockbee gave a dance for the young folks at his home in Harrisonville. This occurred the day after the Confederates had shelled Fort Sumter. At the dance Cole's sister ignored Captain Walley by refusing to dance with him and loudly proclaiming she did not care to do so.

The irate captain took his spite out on Cole by stating the boy was a spy for Quantrill. Colonel Younger made efforts to persuade the boy to attend college at Kansas City, but the boy refused to do so, stating that if he had to fight now was the time.

It was during the winter of 1861 that Cole Younger threw in his fortunes with Quantrill. He was not much more than a boy; but from the first his work and his word were those of a man of high standing. He was the one who refused to kill except in battle or self-defense. Quantrill recognized in him the kind of man who could carry out orders. Numerous times Cole saved the band from annihilation by some clever decision. His presence of mind in untried emergencies made him a calculable asset. He fought as a real soldier, for a cause he believed in, a glory and an ideal.

But Cole's family suffered. Not long after he joined Quantrill's guerrillas, Cole's father was brutally murdered by Federal soldiers. His mother was forced at gun point to set fire to her own home in the dead of winter, and then she had to march through deep snow to the house of a neighbor. Cole's mother was ill with consumption and her case was greatly worsened by this exposure in the bitter cold. It was natural that all this should weigh on Cole Younger's heart and mind and cause him to be one of the best fighters in the Quantrill band. But he was an anomaly among them, for his nature was generous, kind, loyal, he was a man of his word, and he never refused to help a friend.

In 1863 Cole Younger, weary of the seesaw warfare in Missouri, reported for duty to General Henry E. McCulloch at

Bonham, Texas. After doing quite a lot of scout duty for McCulloch, Cole was ordered to report to General E. Kirby Smith at Shreveport, Louisiana. As captain in the Confederate army Cole was told by General Smith to rid the Mississippi River bottoms of the numerous speculators and cotton thieves which infested that area. In February, 1864, Cole was sent to Warren, Arkansas, to report to General John S. Marmaduke (later a Democratic Party Governor of Missouri) on direct orders of General Jo Shelby. His work was so well performed that, in May of the same year, Colonel George S. Jackson was able to lead 300 Confederate cavalrymen across the plains into Colorado to intercept some wagon trains and to cut the transcontinental telegraph wire from Leavenworth to San Francisco. They found the wagon trains deserted. By order from Richmond, Cole Younger was then sent to the Pacific Coast, where he was stationed at the time the war closed.

Frank James also became one of Quantrill's guerrillas under provocation. During the Battle of Wilson's Creek he was captured by Union forces and granted a field parole, which meant that he was to return home and never enlist again on either side. Both governments recognized such paroles, and they were seldom violated, for a soldier's honor went a long way in those days. When Frank returned home, in a nearby town he displayed a huge revolver and boasted that the Yankees had been whipped at Wilson's Creek. He was jailed, and only through the influence of some political friends was his mother able to secure his release. Of course this incident cut Frank to the quick, and he violated his field parole by joining Quantrill. The Jameses were Southern in their beliefs and sympathies, and Frank wanted to fight for the rebel cause. Of course the regular Confederate forces would not let him enlist with them on account of his parole, so he chose the only alternative.

There is no record that the James family was molested prior to Frank's joining Quantrill's raiders, but shortly afterward the Missouri Enrolled State Militia of the Union took every occasion to insult or to beat Jesse, the younger brother of Frank. Their stepfather was hanged and left for dead but was cut down and revived after the soldiers left. Early in 1863 their mother and their sister Susan were arrested and taken to jail in St. Joseph and subjected to insults from the uncouth guards. Susan contracted malaria and almost died. By the time they were released, young Jesse had joined Frank with the guerillas, eager to avenge the harsh treatment he and his family had received.

Some of the depredations committed by Quantrill's men were in retaliation for crimes by the Union General James Lane and Col. Charles R. Jennison's moving bands. Col. Jennison, a former doctor of Leavenworth, Kansas, was commander of the 15th Kansas Volunteer Cavalry. Lane, Burris, Jennison, Peabody, James Montgomery, and Anthony had entered into the border war along with many others, their main purpose was not to subjugate the South but rather to annihilate Quantrill and his band. General Lane had marched his men out of Kansas into Missouri and secured for them all the blue uniforms of the Union Army. They returned to Kansas City with the banner of the United States waving at the head of their column. En route they burned the town of Osceola, Missouri, on September 23, 1861, and drove hundreds of wagonloads of spoils along with them. This incident started a reign of terror and naturally inspired acts of retaliation from the Missouri pro-Confederates who had not forgotten their sufferings from John Brown's raids before the outbreak of the war.

During the summer of 1862 public sentiment was so strong against the authorized Union troops in Missouri that the commanding general at St. Louis called a halt to all official fighting and gave Lane's men a free hand to fight it out with Quantrill. However, it was not long before the Union soldiers were once more in the field, threatened at every turn and at every crossroad by the guerrillas. There is no question but that Quantrill looted and killed others than Union soldiers, usually those whom he suspected of giving aid to or spying for the Union. In Missouri at the time the majority of people sympathized with the South, and in the confusion they were inclined to favor

Quantrill and his men, whom they thought of as defenders of their favorite cause.

The unanimous condemnation of the Federals was intensified by the arrest of Cole Younger's sisters after the murder of their father in 1862 by Union soldiers. The girls had been in the area of the murder and the soldiers were afraid they would testify. Captain Irvin Walley threw them into a dilapidated old jailhouse in Kansas City, at 1409 Grand Avenue. Also incarcerated there were three young sisters of the guerrilla Bill Anderson—Josephine, eighteen, Molly, sixteen, and Janie, ten years old—as well as Mrs. Susan Vandiver, Mrs. Armenia Whitsett-Gilvey, and Mrs. Christie (Charity) Kerr.

These girls and young women were being held pending banishment from Missouri; and when the soldiers discovered that among them were the Anderson girls, they decided to kill them because they bitterly hated Bill Anderson. A Mrs. Duke, who ran a boarding house at Oak Street and Independence Avenue, overheard the soldiers boarding with her make plans to destroy the girls. The plotters didn't realize that Mrs. Duke was a cousin of Bill Anderson, and they made the mistake of letting her hear their decision to undermine the old jail building, instead of burning it, and thus endanger adjoining buildings. They thought it wiser to let the jail cave in on the women prisoners.

Mrs. Duke went into quick action, although not quickly enough to save all the innocent occupants of the rickety old jail. With several of her neighbors she hurried to the military headquarters in Kansas City and pleaded to have the girls removed from the jail. The Commandant did not believe her, or else he himself was in on the plan. At any rate, it was already too late, for while Mrs. Duke was still pleading with the Commandant the undermined building collapsed. Nan Harris (a cousin of Cole Younger, later Mrs. McCorkle) and Molly Anderson were in the hallway when they heard the crash and the agonized screams of the other girls. One of the jail guards, who did not approve of the plot, helped these two to get out of the building to safety. Janie Anderson, the ten-year-old, tried to get out through a window, but there was a large cannonball chained to one of her ankles, so she was helpless. Both her legs were broken. All the other victims went down with the ruins. Josephine Anderson was killed by a pile of bricks that fell on her. Charity Kerr (another cousin of Cole Younger) was killed when a heavy timber struck her. Two other women prisoners who escaped with slight injuries were Miss Molly Cranstaff (later Mrs. William Clay) and Miss Sue Mundy (later Mrs. N. M. Womacks of Blue Springs, Missouri).

The infuriated Bill Anderson, brother of the murdered Josephine, soon became known as Bloody Bill, for he killed fifty-four Union soldiers in revenge. He kept score on a silken cord which he carried in a buckskin pouch, tying a knot for each life taken. It is true that Anderson was ruthless even before the untimely death of his sister; still, there is no doubt that the jail incident strengthened his determination to kill, and after that he spared no Unionist. The watchword along the Kansas-Missouri border became, "Quantrill sometimes spares a life; Anderson never does!"

William Anderson was silent, moody, brooding, in battle a devil incarnate who reveled in daring and danger. He once said, "If I cared for my life I'd have lost it long ago. Wanting to lose it, I can't throw it away." His stamina was amazing, his leadership astounding. He might be surprised by the enemy, but never was he daunted. Wounded or crippled, he fought on, ever more desperately and effectively, recognizing only the law of the gun. His luck finally ran out, though: he was shot dead during a charge in ambush. His body was propped up in a sitting position and photographs were taken of it. Then his head was cut off and put on a spiked telegraph pole.

Some people claimed that it was not Bloody Bill killed that day near Orrick, Missouri, but one of his fellow guerrillas; that Bill Anderson escaped to Texas and lived for another sixty-two years in Brownwood. It is in this town where lie the bones of "Colonel" Henry Ford who, many people thought, was Jesse James, although Ford never laid any claim to that questionable distinction.

CHARACTER STUDIES 59

Not long ago an old photograph was sent to various citizens of Brownwood, and none of them identified the picture as that of the man they had known as Anderson. Prior to his death the Brownwood "Bill Anderson" had applied to the State of Texas for a pension, and at that time the Brown County officials learned that he had arrived there in 1859. Of course he was not the Bloody Bill of guerrilla notoriety, for Bloody Bill actually was killed in Missouri in 1864. It is true that "Brownwood Anderson" was chummy with Ford and Younger, and no doubt all three had at one time or another ridden with Quantrill.

John Thrailkill was another of the guerrillas, a Missourian who turned into a fiend. Before the outbreak of the Civil War, he was a painter engaged to marry a beautiful girl. One night twenty Federal militiamen walked into her home and murdered her invalid father right before her. She lost her reason and soon afterward died. Thrailkill swore death to the militiamen as he reverently kissed the stilled lips of his betrothed. His closest friend was Jesse James, with whom he rode throughout the war years. At the time, however, he joined Quantrill and was personally responsible for the death of eighteen of the twenty soldiers he had vowed to get.

In the summer of 1866 the Governor of Kansas requisitioned the Governor of Missouri for several hundred men, naming those who had taken part in the attack on Lawrence and other Kansas towns during the war. Cole Younger met Jesse James for the first time at Blue Springs, Missouri, while the attorneys at Independence were trying to assemble all the former guerrillas for a meeting, to decide what stand should be taken in regard to the Kansas request. (The Youngers and the Jameses were not cousins as many writers have stated.) But it was found that nothing could legally be done in regard to crimes committed during the war itself. As a result, Missouri did nothing about the burning of Osceola, the Palmyra affair, or other destructive raids.

At the close of the war most of the guerrillas were painted black by contemporary journalists. It was not recognized that a goodly number of the ex-guerrillas had acquitted themselves well after the close of hostilities. Some were elected sheriffs, some representatives in state legislatures, some congressmen; some were appointed judges and county clerks. It would be wearisome to enumerate all the positions of trust held by these same men who had ridden with Quantrill in an effort to help the Southern cause, but many of them did attain to high positions.

The Palmyra Butchery

In a civil war there are of course two factions of the same nation, struggling for supremacy, with only an imaginary state line between them. Men inflamed with passion over the question of freedom or slavery fought not as soldiers for their country, king, ideal, or glory. Intense hatred spurred them on. Savage instincts ran rampant and both sides slaughtered, pillaged, burned, and destroyed without compunction.

Originally the Kansas Redlegs, who wanted their territory admitted to the Union as a free state, had none of this world's goods, whereas their neighbors in Missouri owned slaves and lands and were quite well-to-do. There is no actual record of the first clash between the Kansans and the Missourians which prompted the outbreak of the vicious border warfare, but it is known that livestock and other belongings of the opulent Missouri landowners were constantly missing and were known to have been taken across the border by the poor farmers of Kansas. Raids were started in attempts to recover the stolen goods, and of course these involved killings and more robbery, until the nightmare of guerrilla warfare had evolved.

While the people of Kansas were determined to keep their territory free, the Missourians were equally determined that the new state of Kansas should have slavery, and each side strove strenuously to accomplish its purpose. The leading citizens of Kansas, abolitionists loud in condemning slavery, organized the Immigrant Aid Society, and large numbers of people from other parts of the country came to Kansas under the auspices of this Society. Some of the newcomers proved to be far from desirable neighbors. During the frequent raids it was the practice for each side to rob the other, whether abolitionist or secessionist. This gave rise to the term "Freebooter."

Inasmuch as most writing on Quantrill and his men gives a graphic account of the sacking of Lawrence, Kansas, with little mention of the Palmyra outrage, this is an opportunity to give the full story of that black day. Early in the morning of September 12, 1862, sleepy-eyed Missourians peeked from their windows to see Colonel Joe Porter's company of four hundred gray-clad Confederates dashing down the main street of Palmyra, yelling the old familiar rebel call: "Hurrah for Jeff Davis!"

"To the jail!" commanded Porter. "We've got to rescue our men and get supplies. Don't worry about the Feds holed up in the courthouse—that's a stone building. We'd never take it without artillery."

He was right. Lieutenant Hiram Washburn and his men had taken shelter in several strong brick and stone buildings. Well the Confederates remembered costly instances when they had tried to assault such fortifications with only cavalry troops.

The jail building at Main and Lafayette Streets was surrendered without much firing, and some half a hundred Confederate prisoners were released. But Colonel Porter was sorely disappointed at not getting any much needed supplies. Two hours after their entry into Palmyra the Confederate company departed, taking with them a number of Union prisoners.

"There's a damned Fed!" cried a young corporal as the company passed the store of J. H. Liborious. "Let's give 'im hell!"

Several soldiers fired, but, instead of killing the Union soldier who ran up the nearest alley, they struck the merchant, a staunch Union man and a highly respected citizen.

Colonel Porter's men stopped at Summers' Pasture to decide the fate of their prisoners.

"Where's Captain Shattuck?" asked an aide-de-camp.

"He's on special detail," replied the Colonel. "He'll be along shortly."

Captain J. W. Shattuck had been given the pleasant duty of arresting Andrew Allsman, an elderly resident of Palmyra who had caused Shattuck's arrest and confinement in a Federal prison from which he had recently escaped. Allsman was an undercover Union spy and was most unpopular in the strongly Southern town of Palmyra. Captain Shattuck rushed to the home of Allsman on the north side of the town, ordered the man from his bed, and then rode to join Colonel Porter with his prisoner.

Colonel Porter ordered the prisoners lined up.

"Great heavens! Don't shoot us!" pleaded the ashen-faced Allsman.

The gray-clad officer looked at Allsman with contempt and ordered, "Parole the prisoners. Four shall remain as hostages, among them Allsman."

Had Allsman been permitted to return to Palmyra that morning, one of the blackest crimes of the entire war might have been averted.

The following day the Federal forces of General John McNeil descended on Porter's camp. The Confederates split up into small parties and outwitted the attackers. Allsman had a chance to shift for himself but, panic-stricken, he chose to remain with Captain Shattuck, of all persons. Several days later, Shattuck received orders to meet Colonel Porter at Smith's mill on Troublesome Creek.

Before leaving for this appointment, Captain Shattuck said to his prisoner, "Allsman, I had hoped to take you to Virginia to make you stand fair trial for your crimes against the Confederacy, but now that seems impossible. Since I prefer not to kill an old man, you are free to go."

"Not that, Captain, please! I'd be killed within the hour. One of those men might follow me and kill me."

"All right, then. Come along with me to Troublesome Creek."

When Shattuck reported to Colonel Porter, it was the latter who had the task of disposing of Allsman. He said, "Allsman, you know some of these men. Pick a guard you can trust to escort you to the home of some friend."

Allsman selected six Confederates and left with them. The

next morning this guard returned to report that they had taken Allsman to the place of his choice. Yet Allsman was never heard from again. The general belief was that he had been executed after the guard left him. Some years later a skeleton found near Troublesome Creek was claimed to be that of Allsman, but it showed no bullet holes.

Things hummed in Palmyra, especially in the main saloon. In a far corner sat two Union officers, one well under the effects of liquor. Suddenly he raised a half-filled whisky bottle and threw it across the room. It shattered on the far wall.

"Damn those dirty rebels!" he cried. "General McNeil, we've got to teach them a lesson. An eye for an eye."

"Calm yourself, Colonel Strachan. We'll think this thing out."

"To hell with them. I'm for shooting a number of the citizens in retaliation—Southerners, mind you."

General McNeil showed his impatience with the loud-mouthed colonel. "Come on," he said, "you're going to the barracks. No use making a worse fool of yourself than you already are."

The citizens of Palmyra were afraid to walk in the streets when the rumor of this exchange of ideas drifted from the saloon. But the thought of mass murder reprisals was unthinkable. It is believed that McNeil was persuaded not even to consider such a plan when influential Union citizens met with him.

But on October 8th the hammer fell.

Palmyra, Mo., Oct. 8, 1862

Joseph C. Porter:

Sir: Andrew Allsman, an aged citizen of Palmyra, and a noncombatant, having been carried from his home by a band of persons, unlawfully arraigned against the peace and good order of the State of Missouri, and which band was under your control, this is to notify you that unless said Andrew Allsman is returned to his family within ten days from date, ten men who have belonged to your band, and unlawfully sworn by you to carry arms against the government of the United States, and who now are in custody, will

THE PALMYRA BUTCHERY 65

be shot as a meet reward for their crimes, amongst which is the illegal restraining of said Allsman of his liberty, and if not returned, presumptively aiding in his murder. Your prompt attention to this will save much suffering.

Yours, etc.
W. R. Strachan
Provost Marshal Gen. Dis. N.E. Mo., by order of
Brig. General, Commanding McNeil's Column.

Doubtless the order never reached Colonel Porter who was already in the South; even if it had reached him he would have been powerless to produce Allsman.

Nine days slipped by as one. General McNeil then ordered Provost Marshal Strachan to select the victims among fifty military prisoners at Hannibal and Palmyra. Colonel Strachan selected five men from each town. At the Palmyra prison he brazenly strutted in and announced the names of the five victims from there.

"The men I have called out will be taken to the Fair Grounds tomorrow and executed."

Then with a drunken sneer he walked out of the prison.

Some of the five doomed men were fathers, others had sweethearts, sisters, brothers. With the exception of Willis Baker all of them were young men, in the prime of youth. Rev. J. S. Green visited the condemned men and offered them spiritual consolation. At the closing of the solemn prayer he said, "Forgive those who order this crime, for they know not what they do."

"The hell they don't!" cried the grizzled Willis Baker. "I'm for scratching out that part of the prayer."

It was agreed that Baker was right.

Poor Captain Tom Sidener tried hard to reconcile himself to his fate, but he was handsome, brilliant, and about to be married. His wedding suit was to serve as his death garment. Young Tom had seen gallant service in the cause of the Confederacy, and after the rout of Porter's men at Kirksville had fled to Shelbyville to make his way south. At Shelbyville he had been arrested and sent to the Palmyra military prison.

Morgan Bixler had never borne arms against the Union. His only crime was that he was a Confederate sympathizer. He wrote a touching letter to his wife and two small sons, but the message did not reach them until after his death. Mrs. Bixler had been trying to arrange to visit her husband, but before she could do so his remains were delivered to her. That was the first she knew of his execution.

Eleazer Lake wrote his folks:

Palmyra, Marion County, Mo.
Oct. 17, 1862

Dear Sarah and children: I seat myself to write my last farewell. I am now in jail and have received the sentence of death since dusk. I am to be shot in the morning, but death has no terrors, thank God, as you can see from the hand I write. Bear it with fortitude, for death is only the passage from earth to Heaven, and I feel prepared to go. We shall all soon meet in Heaven, where all tears will be wiped away, and where parting will be no more, and where sickness and sorrow never come. Dear, do not distress about it more than you can avoid. I shall like to see you all once more, but we will meet in another world. I bid my friends farewell, and you, dear wife and children, praying God may bless, protect and support you through your trials.

These men were reputable citizens of Missouri: Willis Baker, Thomas Humston, Morgan Bixler, John Y. McPheeters, Herbert Hudson, John M. Wade, Marion Lair, Captain Thomas A. Sidener, Eleazer Lake, and William T. Humphrey. They had never been guerrillas under Quantrill as McNeil implied. Some of them had broken their parole oath never again to bear arms against the United States. Most of them were farmers who hated war but who had been conscripted into the Union army and so had chosen to join Porter. They had felt that if they had to fight they would rather be on the side where their sympathies lay.

Late Friday night before the executions a prominent merchant stepped into Nicol's undertaking parlors.

"What goes, Sam—working late?"

"Rush order. General McNeil says he's got to have ten coffins by tomorrow morning."

"Then that devil's threat is true. He intends to murder ten men tomorrow."

Sam said, "Looks like it," and continued with his work.

His visitor said no more but left the building, his head bowed in silent prayer. Unwillingly he now had to convey the horrible message to the rest of Palmyra. Prominent citizens tried to appeal to General McNeil, but the drunken Strachan intercepted them, saying that the general was too busy to see them and shrugging his shoulders.

"They are getting what they deserve," he said. "I don't give a damn if every Southern rebel in Palmyra is cut up and floated down the river."

With that he took another long drag from his whiskey bottle and slammed the door of his quarters.

Mrs. Mary Humphrey came to Strachan to plead for her husband. She told him that her husband had refused ever again to take up arms, that he had never violated his parole—but it was of no use. Strachan laughed in her face, his whiskey breath almost causing her to faint.

Federal Captain Thacker knew that he had incurred Strachan's hatred by his liberal treatment of all prisoners, so he did not try to interfere. But he suggested that Mrs. Humphrey make a point of reaching General McNeil. When she did so he showed no interest.

"Your husband has been chosen and must die, Mrs. Humphrey. I am sorry. Good day," was all he said.

The horrified woman returned to the home of a relative in town. She gathered her nine-year-old stepdaughter into her arms and sobbed, "Sally, you've got to go to General McNeil, plead with him that your father was in Palmyra when Porter's men attacked."

The pitiful pleas of the child finally reached the stone heart of McNeil. He scratched a quick note and handed it to Captain Reed, with instructions that it be delivered to Colonel Strachan with the utmost speed.

In a drunken stupor the Provost Marshal read the note aloud:

Col. Strachan: If the fact can be established that Humphrey was in Palmyra when Porter came here and refused to leave with him, reprieve him, and put no one in his place.

Strachan flew into a blind rage. "That damned fool McNeil! To hell with him. Ten coffins have been made, and ten coffins will be filled."

"If you demand a tenth man," suggested Captain Reed, "take one without a family."

"An idea. Come, let's go to the jail."

The attentive jailer snapped to attention. What was this? Surely not more men to be condemned? Into the prison strutted Colonel Strachan, in his wake the sympathetic captain.

"Hiram Smith!" Strachan snapped.

The twenty-one-year-old youth was seated in the cell of Willis Baker, trying to comfort the old man, little knowing what was in store for himself.

"You're Hiram Smith?" demanded Strachan. "You are notified herewith that you are to share the same fate as your companions here and the men from Hannibal."

"I fear not death," said the youth. "Do what you will."

Mrs. Humphrey could hardly believe that her husband had been spared, and while she rejoiced she did not know that another had been chosen to die in his place. Nor did she know the horrible price she would have to pay before her husband could get his release.

Hiram Smith prepared for his death by writing this letter:

Palmyra, Mo., Oct. 18, 1862.
Military Prison

Dear Sister: I seat myself for the last time to write you a few lines. A sentence was read to me a few moments ago that I am to be shot at 1 o'clock this evening, and all that I can say is goodbye, sisters, brothers, and friends. Tell my brothers what is going to become of me. Tell them goodbye for me. I never expect to meet them in this world any more, but hope to meet you all beyond this

THE PALMYRA BUTCHERY 69

vale of tears, where parting is no more. So farewell, brothers and sisters, I want you to kiss the little children for me. So farewell, my dear brothers and sisters, for the last time on earth. I remain,
Your affectionate brother,
Hiram Smith.

Shortly after noon on Saturday, October 18, 1862, three military wagons pulled up in front of the jail. Two wagons carried three coffins each, the other four. The ten condemned men were marched from the jail and placed on the wagons, each seated upon his own coffin. A cordon of soldiers surrounded the wagons as they started the death march down Main Street. From Main Street the silent group made its way south to Jefferson Street, then turned east to the fairgrounds near the eastern limits of the town. The route was lined with silent mourners who dared not openly express their feelings.

The ten coffins were arranged in a row about six feet apart. The doomed men now realized that nothing would occur to prevent the carrying out of the sentence. McNeil and the monster from Shelby County, Colonel Strachan, had preceded the group to the grounds, but the general had returned to his quarters, leaving Strachan in charge.

"Take your positions in front of your coffins," Strachan ordered. "Your names are scrawled on them."

The ten men seated themselves on the coffins and bravely waited for the musket fire of the thirty Federal soldiers. They refused blindfolds and sat erect.

"Ready!" cried Strachan. "Aim! Fire!"

The calm afternoon air was rent by the mighty roar of the muskets, but the soldiers had been nervous—they were used to honorable combat, not murdering prisoners. Many bullets struck buildings to the rear of the condemned men. Three of them were killed outright. Morgan Bixler had not been hit at all but the others were weltering in their blood. Major Dodson had received orders to compel many of the citizens to witness the ceremony, and now the spectators gaped in horror at the sickening scene.

Some of the soldiers hurried among the fallen men, firing as they walked. Bullet after bullet was fired into the bodies until it was certain all were dead. The bodies were roughly thrown into the coffins and carted back to town.

John McPheeters' brother approached Colonel Strachan and asked permission to claim John's body.

"Take the whole goddamned lot of them if you like. They're good for nothing but fertilizer now, and poor stuff at that."

The coffins were thrown off the wagons in front of the courthouse. By evening all except three had been claimed by friends and relatives. Those three were buried by the soldiers but later were claimed by members of the families when the news reached them.

The fairgrounds were never used again, for that terrible deed had hallowed the place with the blood of heroes and innocent men.

For many years the remains of Hiram T. Smith rested in an unmarked grave in a lonely cemetery in Lewis County. But today there is a marker:

HIRAM SMITH
This Monument is Dedicated
to the Memory of
HIRAM T. SMITH
Who Was Shot at Palmyra
October 18, 1862,
As a Substitute for
WILLIAM T. HUMPHREY,
My Father.

All sorts of rumors filled Palmyra after the deaths of these victims of Strachan's wrath. Humphrey had not yet been released, and his wife feared he had been spared only to be shot at a later date. Others claimed that McNeil was planning to shoot ten citizens each week until Allsman was returned.

Mrs. Humphrey hurried to Colonel Strachan's office, where she found him in a drunken stupor. Possibly he was trying to let whiskey drown the memory of that black Saturday. He in-

THE PALMYRA BUTCHERY 71

sisted that for her husband's release Mrs. Humphrey would have to submit herself to his lust. She was under such a mental strain that she consented, hardly knowing what she was doing.

Goaded by the world-wide accusations of brutality as a result of the killings at the fairgrounds, Provost Marshal William R. Strachan on December 10, 1862, addressed the Editor of the *New York Times*:

> Sir: Noticing in your issue of December 1 an extended extract from foreign papers, accompanied by an editorial, upon the execution of ten rebels at this place, which extract and editorial appear based upon an entire misconstruction of the facts of the case, and thereby casting grave censure upon a meritorious officer, I am led (having by position at the time an opportunity of knowing everything conected with the transaction), out of regard to the truth of history, and to do justice to General McNeil, to address you on the subject. It is very difficult for men removed thousands of miles from the scene of action—men who are placed in a locality where law and order prevail, where loyalty is universal—to begin even to appreciate slightly the deep malice, the enormous crimes, the treacheries, the assassinations, the perjuries that invariably have characterized those, especially in Missouri, who have taken up arms avowedly to destroy their Government.
>
> Now, Mr. Editor, here in Missouri our Government commenced by extending toward the rebels in our midst every kindness, and a degree of clemency that soon caused it to be much safer, in every part of our State, to be a rebel than to be a Union man. Every neighborhood was coerced, whilst the Government was maintaining with the State a large force, at no time less than 50,000 men, and often largely over-running those figures. Still treason continued rampant, traitors publicly held forth on the clemency with which they were treated, regarding it as proof and confession of the weakness of the Government, that she dare not hurt any one. Union men and their families were forced to leave their homes and their all and fly for protection and for life to the loyal States. I have seen hundreds of wagons on their way to Illinois and other States—families who had lived in independent circumstances forced to live on corn-meal and water and beg their way along. The Union troops, by their kindness, were absolutely offering a premium to

treason and crime. Their presence, under the orders they were forced to act on, became, instead of protection, absolutely a terrible evil. Union men dared not give the troops information; assassination was sure to follow. Things went on from bad to worse. Soon the scoundrels began the innocent pastime of shooting into passenger-cars, of burning railroad bridges, not as a military necessity, but for the sole purpose of murder. Hundreds of non-combatants were crippled and murdered—wives made insane by the enormous outrages they committed. Some of the men perpetrating these hideous crimes were caught. I participated in the action of the commission appointed to try them. They were proved guilty and sentenced to be shot . . . that sentence . . . not carried out to this day. Some of these miscreants have even been turned loose once more. Such clemency proved to be the most horrid cruelty. The unfortunates of our State who, in their heart of hearts, held that loyalty to their Government was a sacred and holy duty that they could not cast aside, began to look at one another in surprise and horror. Will our Government never understand our situation? Will it continue to strengthen the cause of the robbers and murderers? What is to become of us? Stout-hearted men, whose families would not permit of leaving, sat down in the midst of their household goods and shed tears of hopeless agony. . . .

I could give a long list of crimes the most horrid committed by these scoundrels, that would make even fiends in hell shudder. Their robberies and devastations you, in New York, cannot even conceive of; but when I say there were thousands upon thousands of these men; that they had no money; that they subsisted wholly by robbery, you may approximate toward an estimate; and all this in a State that refused to secede from the Union, hundreds of miles inside the Federal lines. General McNeil with a small force was pursuing them, not like the advance of a force in all the "pomp and circumstance of glorious war," but at the rate of 45 miles per day, often camping at 10 p.m., and breaking camp at 2 a.m. . . .

In the particular case of Andrew Allsman, he was a man upward of sixty years of age, taken from his family and murdered. Of the ten men executed, one of them was one of the party who murdered Mr. Pratt. . . . The other nine men were all caught with arms, and all of them had been once pardoned for their former treason by taking the oath of allegiance to the United States, and had deliberately perjured themselves by going out again—the very oath they took expressly stipulating that "death would be the penalty for a violation of this their solemn oath and parole of honor." Now, sir, are such men entitled to the consideration of honorable warfare (as you seem to think in your criticisms), or are they not rather to be treated as outlaws and beyond the pale of civilization? And, sir, living as we do in Missouri, in times of red revolution, assassination, rapine, in violation of all laws, both human and divine, acts of justice necessarily assume the garb of severity, and the more severe to the criminal the more merciful to the community.

Mr. Editor, if you could have been a witness to many scenes that attended General McNeil's visit to the various posts of his districts, made but two weeks since, when he traversed the whole country on horseback, attended but by two orderlies, when old men would come out of their farm houses, shake hands with the general, call down blessings upon him, ask him to delay so that their wives could come out and thank him for executing justice. . . .

These terrible "butcheries" (i.e., the just punishing of guerrillas, assassins, and violators of parole) have finally restored safety here. Since the public execution of the ten men at Palmyra, not a murder nor a single personal outrage to a Union man has been committed in Northeastern Missouri. . . .

But in spite of Strachan's eloquent plea for public sympathy with his viewpoint, the horror of that Saturday execution hurt the Union cause at home and abroad. The story of it circled the globe.

President Lincoln discussed it with his Cabinet. But McNeil fortified himself with signatures of numerous Missourians endorsing the affair, no doubt many of them obtained under threat. McNeil's immediate superior officers justified him by claiming that Colonel Porter had no authority to recruit soldiers for the Confederacy and that his men were nothing but guerrillas, bandits, and murderers. They cited incidents perpetrated by Quantrill's men and attributed them to Porter.

Strachan soon left Palmyra for his home in Shelby County. A year later he was court-martialed for his part in the Palmyra affair, but he received only a year's sentence and did not serve that. In his behalf General McNeil appealed to General Rosecrans, who was easily convinced that Strachan was a victim of prejudice. Strachan was pardoned, and in February, 1866, he died in New Orleans, friendless and penniless.

McNeil resided in St. Louis for the rest of his life. The specter of Palmyra followed him wherever he went and in whatever he did. In 1880 his nomination for the office of United States Marshal failed to be confirmed by the Senate. When he ran for Auditor of St. Louis in 1889, the newspapers reviewed the Palmyra butchery, and he was defeated. He died in June, 1891.

Battles of Carthage and Wilson's Creek

The original members of Quantrill's band, which was formed during the winter of 1860, were William Haller, James and John Little, Edward Goger, Andrew Walker, John Hampton, James Kelly, and Solomon Basham. The severe weather made it impossible for them to secure supplies and recruits, so the men remained in camp almost the entire time, making plans and setting up what was to be an effective means of communication between themselves and their many friends.

The keen mind of Quantrill foresaw a gigantic struggle in the near future, and his thought was to get ready for it. Ostensibly forming his group for retaliation raids against the Kansas Jayhawkers, Quantrill was laying plans to seek revenge against his self-believed Kansas enemies. The guerrilla leader was a good talker, yet he found it difficult to recruit fighters to carry on his personal battles. However, with the outbreak of the Civil War in April of 1861 things took on a different outlook. By the spring of 1861 Quantrill had managed to swell his ranks by the enlistment of David Pool, John Jarrette, William Gregg, John Koger, Richard Burns, George Todd, and George Shepherd.

Quantrill led these fifteen men to participate in the Battle of Carthage, Missouri (sometimes referred to as the Battle of Dry Forks), on July 5, 1861. It was the first important encounter of armed forces in Missouri.

At the outbreak of the war Governor Claiborne F. Jackson of Missouri took to the field in the uniform of a Confederate general. At Carthage General Franz Sigel assured his Federal batteries that there would be no serious conflict; that a few rounds of grape and canister fired into the midst of the Missourians would quickly disperse them. He was due for a big surprise.

Since it seemed impossible for General Jackson to get his Confederate cavalry and guerrilla aids in position under Sigel's fire, he issued the order for the infantry to charge the enemy and the cavalry to come up at the same time in supporting distance. As a result, the Federals retreated across Bear Creek, a wide and deep stream, destroying a bridge at their passing. About a mile beyond the creek they took a stand behind a skirt of timber.

Before Jackson's men could attack, they would have to cross an open field while exposed to a raking fire. The cavalry, including Quantrill and his men, dismounted and advanced with the infantry. They threw a lot of timber into the stream and crossed over. After an hour's hard fighting, the Federals abandoned their position and hurried to Carthage, fighting as they ran. Here they made another stand, forming ambuscades behind every available cover. When darkness fell, General Sigel and his soldiers fell back to Rolla, Missouri—about forty miles from the scene of the first fighting that day, where Sigel had expected so little trouble.

At Carthage, Quantrill was under the immediate command of Captain Stewart's cavalry, and Cole Younger was serving in the State Guard, not yet having joined Quantrill. The official record describes the battle in this way:

> Union, 3rd and 5th Missouri, one battery of the Missouri Artillery. Confed., Mo., State Guard and supplements. Losses, Union, 13 killed, 31 wounded. Confed. 30 killed, 125 wounded, 45 prisoners.

The Battle of Wilson's Creek (or Oak Hill), Missouri, occurred more than a month later, on August 10, 1861. In this Frank James was fighting under General Sterling Price in the State (C.S.A.) Militia. Quantrill also was there, and he did some spectacular fighting, always getting out in front with his blazing red shirt, creating a target for all the enemy. He escaped injury only by some rare stroke of luck.

BATTLES OF CARTHAGE AND WILSON'S CREEK 77

The previous day General Benjamin McCulloch (brother of General Henry E. McCulloch) and his forces had arrived at Wilson's Creek intending to advance upon the Union forces at Springfield. But the Federal General Nathaniel Lyon had anticipated McCulloch's move, so he advanced General Sigel to the right flank while he himself took the left. McCulloch sent forward Colonel A. Hebert's Louisiana Volunteers and Colonel L. McIntosh's mounted Arkansans, and these men, moving to the left, gained a position along a fence that enclosed a cornfield. Here McIntosh dismounted his men and, with Hebert's regiment, advanced in a terrible conflict of small arms while Sigel's artillery played havoc among them. At a critical moment General McCulloch himself led a charge, while McIntosh and Hebert brought up their men, with the result that Sigel's forces fell back in confusion.

The Confederates captured a number of cannon. Having cleared the rear and right, McCulloch now concentrated his fire at the center where the gallant General Lyon was pressing with all his strength. Along the entire line of the hill upon which the Confederates were posted, a raking fire of musketry was kept up. Masses of infantry attacked, fell back, and attacked again. Captain Toten's Union battery perpetrated slaughter among Price's and McCulloch's men. Then Reid's battery was brought up and Hebert's Louisiana regiment was again called into action on the left of it.

It was evident by this time that General Lyon's Unionists were falling back, so Lyon called to his men that he himself would lead a final charge. He had advanced but a little way when two balls pierced his breast, and he fell dead from his horse. The Federal line pushed forward, but they staggered before the reserves thrown in by McCulloch and Price. At last the Federal center gave way. Soon the Federal infantry columns, artillery, and wagons were seen in the distance, rapidly retreating toward Springfield—defeated and driven from the field, harassed all along the way by Quantrill and his guerrillas.

For the Confederates that Battle of Wilson's Creek was one of the most brilliant victories, and it afforded the Missourians an opportunity to assemble a grand campaign under the Stars and Bars. However, even during this battle Price and McCulloch had been arguing about which of them should be in command. McCulloch insisted he ought to command both his troops and Price's, since he was a regular commissioned Confederate General and Price was only a General of the State Militia at that time.* Now they could not agree on a campaign. Therefore McCulloch returned to Arkansas with his men.

The official record for the Battle of Wilson's Creek follows:

Union, 6th and 10th Missouri Cavalry. 2nd Kansas Mounted Volunteers. One company of 1st U.S. Calvary, 1st Iowa, 1st Kansas, 2nd, 3rd, and 5th Missouri. Detachments of 1st and 2nd U.S. Regulars, Missouri Home Guards, 1st Missouri Light Artillery, Battery F 2nd U.S. Artillery.

Confederate, 1st, 3rd, 4th and 5th Missouri State Guard, Graves' Infantry, Bledsoe's Battery, Cawthorn's Brigade, Kelly's Infantry, Brown's Calvary, Burbridge's Infantry, 1st Cavalry, Hughes', Thornton's, Wingo's, Foster's Infantry, Rives', Campbell's Cavalry, 3rd, 4th, 5th Arkansas, 1st Cavalry, Woodruff's, Reid's Battery, 1st, 2nd, Mounted Riflemen, Mountain Volunteers, South Kansas—Texas Mounted Regiment, 3rd Louisiana.

Losses, Union, 223 killed, 721 wounded, 291 missing. Brig. Gen. Nathaniel Lyon was among those killed.

Confederacy, 265 killed, 800 wounded, 30 missing.

It was because of Frank James's part in this fight that he got into trouble. After it was over, back home in Kearney, Mis-

---

*Later, as Major-General in the regular Confederate Army, Price commanded the Army of the West; still later, he commanded a corps of Van Dorn's Army of Mississippi. He held various commands in Arkansas and elsewhere. His most noteworthy effort was the expedition into Missouri from August to December of 1864, to recruit large numbers from the independent bands in that state before Rosecrans drove him back into Arkansas. After the war, Price became temporarily interested in a colonization scheme in Mexico, but he returned to St. Louis in 1866 during an epidemic which caused his death on September 29, 1867.

souri, he talked rather loudly about how "we whipped the Yankees there." That was the occasion, as already mentioned, when he was arrested by the Federal militia and confined at Liberty, Missouri. Through the efforts of his mother, he was released upon his promise never again to take up arms against the United States. Later he decided to ignore this promise and joined Quantrill's guerrilla forces.

Battle of Lexington

Quantrill had made a reputation for himself at Wilson's Creek because of his prominent fighting and his reckless bravery with his bright-red shirt standing out in the first rank of every advance. People spoke of the fact that he had always been the last man to fall back when the order to retreat was given. Cole Younger, too, under the Confederate State Militia, had been outstanding in that battle.

No longer discounting the strength of the enemy, on the 12th of September General Price approached Lexington, Missouri, with his Confederate following. In the center of the town stood the College Building, a large brick structure, and it was here that the defending Colonel James A. Mulligan had raised an earthwork ten feet high, with a ditch eight feet wide, enclosing the college within an area sufficient to hold a garrison of ten thousand men.

Mulligan and his Irish Brigade had been rushed up from Jefferson City to assist in the defense of Lexington, and he was well entrenched. Nevertheless, his garrison had not stocked a sufficient supply of water, and they had to make running fights for it to the river a half mile distant, then fight their way back. During these skirmishes Quantrill exercised his daring, cutting off Union soldiers whenever he could.

As Price approached Lexington, he had several skirmishes with guard detachments of the Union outpost, and it was rumored that a general assault was about to take place just outside the town. This did not develop; but, after two unsuccessful attacks against the fortified college, General Price withdrew his men to encampment because most of their ammunition was depleted and they could do nothing more until his ammunition train arrived.

BATTLE OF LEXINGTON

While a detachment of the Missouri Confederate Fourth Division, under Colonel A. B. Rives substituting for General Slack, was en route to capture a steamboat lying under the enemy guns, they were fired upon from the Anderson House which was marked as a hospital. It is true that this building housed twenty-four sick persons, but also inside it were a large number of Union soldiers. Quickly several companies from Brigadier General Thomas A. Harris' command rushed to the Anderson building and captured it. They now were in control of an important position, for it was within one hundred yards of the Union entrenchments.*

The morning of September 19, 1861, a steady cannon bombardment of the besieged garrison was begun. The incessant rain of shot and shell was bringing death and injury, and the men were also suffering from thirst. On the 20th, General Price brought up a number of bales of hemp and hastily constructed movable breastworks. Several daring sorties were made by the Union men to drive back Price's men, but finally Colonel Mulligan saw that his position was hopeless, so he surrendered.

The fruits of this victory brought joy to the Confederates as well as great quantities of ammunition, food supplies—and money. They recovered a million dollars in gold and silver coins which had been taken from the Lexington Bank in accordance with Major General John C. Fremont's instructions. General Price now ordered this money restored to the owners.

The Union losses were heavy: 42 killed, 108 wounded, 1624 missing and captured. The Confederate losses were light in comparison: 25 killed, 75 wounded.

After Lexington, Quantrill went with the command as far as the Osage River, and there, with the consent of his officers,

---
*Today the Anderson House is a museum visited each year by thousands of tourists. The old bullet holes can still be seen in the walls, and there are hiding places inside the building, from which Union soldiers were taken prisoners. In May, 1955, the Battle of Lexington was re-enacted on the grounds where it was originally fought.

moved up the Kansas Line again to settle some old scores with the forces of Lane and Jennison. Now it was the autumn of 1861, and his band had dwindled to a mere dozen members. They first brushed with Jennison's forces at Morgan Walker's where they ambushed some Jayhawkers, killing six of them. Quantrill next struck at a small band of Missouri Militia near the home of Volney Ryan, also a militiaman.

Next, in Jackson County, the guerrillas killed a man named Searcy. Quantrill had learned from his civilian spies that Searcy was stealing right and left, all through that county, and resorting to violence at times to enforce his demands. On a crisp fall morning of 1861, Quantrill and his men took Searcy from his home and hanged him. Many stolen items were recovered from his home and returned to the former owners wherever possible, even some of the horses Searcy had stolen.

Shortly after this hanging, Cole Younger joined the Quantrill band, which had now swelled in numbers to almost fifty expert riflemen ready to exact vengeance on the Federals for various real and fancied wrongs. On November 10, 1861, they attacked eighty-five millitiamen in the vicinity of Independence, Misouri, on the Charles Younger place, and succeeded in disposing of a dozen or more of them before the rest ran in panic to the protection of their main division in Independence. Had it not been for the other soldiers in the town, Colonel Burris' entire detachment would probably have been wiped out that day.

General Jim Lane, in command of all the Kansas Militia, sent Captain Peabody with a company into Missouri to capture or destroy Quantrill and his band. Their trail was not hard to follow. On January 3, 1862, in Jackson County the Federal troops reached the country home of one John Flannery, where their quarry had bedded down for the night. In short order the Federals surrounded the house and demanded the immediate surrender of the guerrillas. Quantrill asked for a fifteen-minute parley with his men, then yelled defiantly and opened fire. Captain Peabody's aide was killed in the first barrage from the house, and immediately a fierce fight was in progress.

Peabody had no artillery and could only send round after round of rifle and revolver fire into the windows and walls of the building. This continued for more than an hour. Then the Federals piled dry straw to the rear of the house where there were no windows, and quickly gigantic leaping flames were crackling and licking at the walls.

Quantrill and his men rigged up dummies from pillows and bedclothing and put them near the windows where they could be seen by the soldiers. Due to the thick smoke and the late hour, the trick enabled the besieged guerrillas to bolt through the front door, firing as they went with every weapon they had. Cole Younger, as rear guard, displayed remarkable nerve. Two of the guerrillas who had refused to make the break for freedom stayed and perished in the flames. It was learned later that eighteen of the Federals were killed and about twenty wounded.

As was their custom, the guerrillas separated for several days in order to throw off pursuit, but they met later at a designated place. All that winter, Independence was a scene of bloody warfare. Burris' command stayed barricaded in the courthouse. One day early in February, 1862, Quantrill rode into town with David Pool, Bill Gregg, George Shepherd, and Cole Younger, and they charged in pairs down the main street toward the courthouse, with other members of their band racing into town on other streets. Eleven of the guerrillas were wounded, but a much-needed supply of ammunition was obtained in this daring surprise raid. Seven militiamen were killed.

At daybreak of February 21st, Quantrill's gang again invaded the town of Independence, but this time the Federals were ready for them. Instead of only one company, four companies greeted the guerrillas. There was a brief but fierce skirmish in which seventeen of the Union soldiers were killed, and one guerrilla later died of wounds.

On the first day of March Quantrill decided once more to attack Independence, this time in greater force. His guerrillas met at David George's home and rode toward the town as far as

Little Blue Church, where Allen Parmer, later the husband of Jesse James' sister Susan, informed them that the number of Jayhawkers at Independence had now increased from 300 to 600. Quantrill considered these odds briefly and postponed the attack. He and his gang swung around and took a road that led southwest.

When they reached the bridge at Big Blue River, they killed the thirteen soldiers guarding it and destroyed the bridge. They then rode on and had supper at the home of Alexander Majors. Nightfall found Quantrill and twenty-one of his men at the Tate home near the town of New Santa Fe in Jackson County, where they were to spend the bitter cold night. Todd and the remaining guerrillas found lodging five miles farther north.

A militia command 300 strong rode out from town to capture the guerrillas, spies having reported where they were. It was nearly midnight when Quantrill, Jarrette, and Cole Younger heard their sentry challenge the soldiers. The Federals had gotten so close that the guard was forced to flee into the nearby woods before he could sound the alarm to the occupants of the house. There came a loud pounding on the front door, followed by a harsh demand for admittance. Quantrill fired through the panel of the door and the visitor fell dead. The fight then began in earnest. Volley after volley of gunfire poured against the building with many of the Minié balls coming right through the walls.

Quantrill admitted to his men that they were in a serious plight and said that anyone wishing to surrender could accompany the Tate family into the Federal lines, since the Union commander had announced he would allow the members of the family safe passage. Four of the guerrillas accepted this way out. Of course the Federals were only too glad to get the Tates out of the besieged house, for now they could fire the ell as they had done at the Flannery house.

As the flames began to mount, Quantrill ordered shotguns to the front, men with revolvers to bring up the rear. The guerrillas, led by their undaunted chieftain, went dashing out of the burning house, cutting a path for themselves through the lines of blue-uniformed men, their guns and pistols dealing death as they ran. One of the guerrillas named Hoy was captured and taken to Leavenworth, Kansas, where he was later hanged. It seems a miracle that only one of the band was taken during that charge.

In the meantime Todd and his company, from where they had gone for the night, heard the firing at the Tate house. They saddled up and galloped to the scene. On the way they met about a hundred militiamen and, after a fierce fight, had to seek shelter in the woods. It was later learned that the four guerrillas who had surrendered to the Federals at the Tate house, on being promised their lives, had informed about Todd and his contingent several miles ahead. The soldiers Todd and his men met had been dispatched from the Tate house with orders to exterminate them.

Quantrill and his men managed to escape on foot from the Tate house, the darkness of night and the adjacent wooded country being in their favor. When they had walked about three miles, they ambushed thirteen Federal soldiers, shot them to death, and took their horses.

On March 22, 1862, Quantrill and his irregulars attacked Independence (or Little Santa Fe) which was held by the Second Kansas Cavalry detachment. In the fight, the Union loss was one killed, two wounded; while Quantrill lost seven men.

April of 1862 found him with about twenty of his men camped at the house of Sam Clark, near Stony Point in Jackson County. On a bright spring morning Captain Peabody charged upon them with a strong detachment of Federal cavalry. Quickly the Quantrill men took refuge in the house and in a nearby smokehouse. In those days Missouri was extensively timbered, and the wooded area was close to the various farm buildings.

Sheltered in the woods, the Federals kept up a long-range duel while Captain Peabody sent to Pink Hill for reinforcements. At first the Federals had used their revolvers, then they had begun firing with carbines. Some of the soldiers crept closer and poured an incessant fire into the house and smokehouse. Captain Peabody knew who the men were inside and was determined to make every effort to take them, alive or otherwise.

Cornered, pressed hard, Quantrill decided on a daring move. Although a vicious scoundrel, he certainly was not lacking in courage. In any emergency he thought straight and fast. His tactic now was to draw the fire of the enemy and give his own men a chance to cut the enemy down.

After making this decision, Quantrill ran alone from the house to the smokehouse, and from there back into the house, deliberately drawing the fire of the soldiers. Being so eager to kill the daring guerrilla chieftain, the Federals exposed themselves unduly and were killed by the return fire from the guerrillas. Presently the entire band of Quantrill's men dashed for the dense woods and safety.

The Federals fired one volley from their carbines at the fast-fleeing guerrillas, then grabbed their revolvers; but to their chagrin they found they had failed to reload the revolvers after the first charge, and the guerrillas all escaped. (It is easy to understand that the Union soldiers, in the excitement, naturally plunged their revolvers back into the holsters instead of taking time in that moment of stress to reload them. Don't forget that the pistols of that day were cap-and-ball percussion-type weapons.)

Quantrill decided to ambush the reinforcements from Pink Hill in order to get more horses for his band. He and his men hurried to a small bluff overlooking a winding creek where the troops stopped to let their horses drink. Suddenly a rain of lead struck from above. Utterly taken by surprise, the soldiers stood with their mouths gaping, hardly offering any resistance, for they had been so sure that the guerrillas were being held at bay in the Clark home near Stony Point. Quantrill later stated that he killed all these soldiers in retaliation for Peabody's burning of Clark's buildings. However, there was actually no reason for his making an excuse, since it was war, and each side was out to get the other. Besides, his excuse fell on deaf ears, since almost everyone knew that he never took prisoners and never overlooked an opportunity to exterminate Union soldiers.

COLE YOUNGER
Pistol

TO WHOM IT MAY CONCERN:

We, the undersigned, do hereby certify that the following described pistol belonged to Cole Younger, a member of the famous "James Gang" of outlaws and robbers; (1) Colt "Frontier" Model 1875 pistol, nickle plated, 45 caliber, 7½ inch barrel, Serial # 70432. Barrel of gun shows evidence of having been struck by bullet. This will substantiate the story of Younger himself that this gun was shot from his hand and ejector knocked off, during the bank hold-up at Northfield, Minnesota, September 21, 1876.

We further certify that this pistol was given to the late Thomas T. Crittenden Jr., after Younger had been released from the penitentiary in Minnesota and came to live in Lees Summit, Missouri. Cole Younger stated when giving the pistol to Mr. Crittenden, it had been used in many of the raids "pulled" by the James Gang.

Mrs Thomas T Crittenden Jr.
Mrs. Thomas T. Crittenden Jr.,
Widow of late Thomas T. Crittenden Jr., to whom Younger gave gun.

Mason Crittenden Stout
Mason Crittenden Stout
Daughter of late Thomas T. Crittenden Jr., and who remembers the gift.

State of Missouri)
County of Jackson) ss

Before me, the undersigned authority, on this day personally appeared Mrs. Thomas T. Crittenden Jr., and Mrs. Mason Crittenden Stout who are known to me to be the persons whose names are subscribed to the foregoing instrument, and acknowledged to me that they executed the same.
Given Under My Hand and Seal of Office at Kansas City, Mo., on this, the 3rd day of Sept , A. D. 19 38 .

John C Slate
Notary

Copy of the Affidavit covering the Cole Younger Gun.

Mrs. Caroline C. Quantrill, mother of Wm. C. Quantrill, the once famous bushwhacker and guerilla leader, is a guest of Mrs. Zuelda Samuels, mother of the famous Jessie James, at Mrs. Samuel's home near Liberty, Mo. The occasion has been made a sort of family reunion. Mrs. Samuels and Mrs. Quantrill have a friendly feeling for each other, owing to the similar experiences of their boys. They talk for hours about the members of their families. Both of them had good husbands who were men of character and education. Mrs. Quantrill's husband was a college professor, and Mrs. Samuel's first husband, Rev. Robert James, was a schoolmaster and a respected minister. Jessie James' grave is in the corner of the yard, and the spot is well cared for by a mother's hand. On a tree that stands near the front gate still hangs the sign: "All strangers 25 cents admittance."

This article is taken from an old faded copy of the Menardville Monitor (now known as Menard, Texas,) which was published by W. C. Reinman, and the date is November 10, 1883.

James Younger

Coleman Younger

Rare photo of Sam Hildebrand never before published.

General James H. Lane.

Colonel Upton S. Hays.

Captain John Jarrette.

Captain William H. Gregg.

Lee McMurtry and
William Hulse.

The watch Quantrill carried throughout the Civil War. Now the property of T. O. Cramer, Kansas City, Missouri.

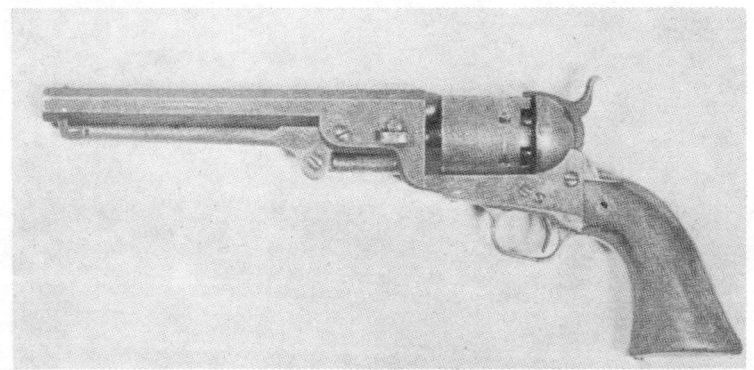

Colt's percussion Navy, serial 51010, William Arny presented to John Brown and Brown later returned to Arny. *Kansas State Historical Society.*

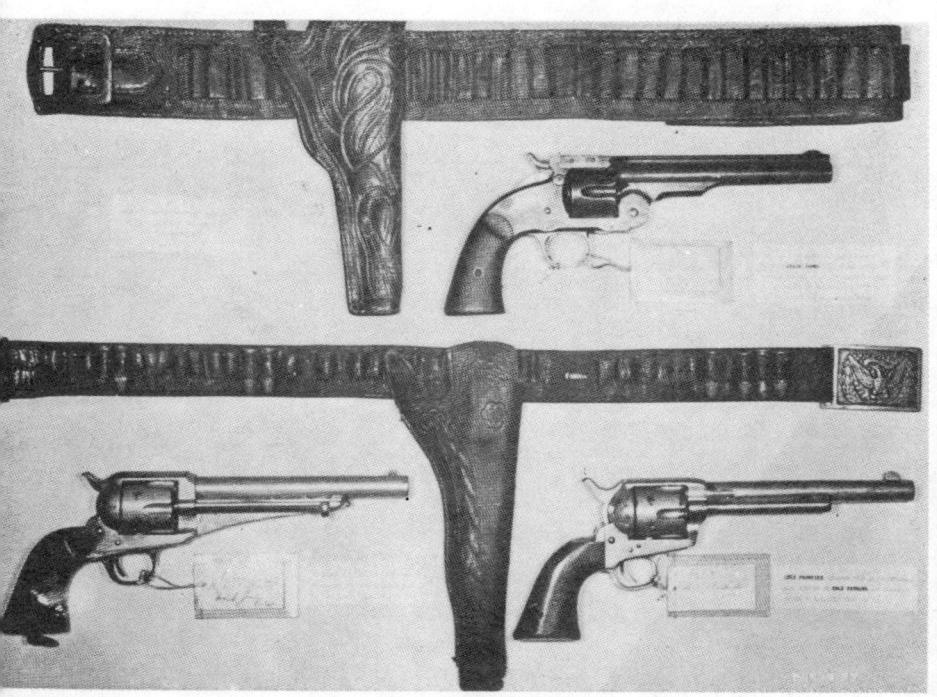

Upper: Gun and holster which Jesse James placed on the bed the day he was killed. This is a Smith & Wesson, Schofield model, .45 calibre, serial 366, 1873. Center and lower left: Gun and holster which Frank James surrendered to Governor T. T. Crittenden, October 1882. This is a Remington Frontier .44 calibre, nickel plated, serial 15116. Lower right: Revolver given to Governor Crittenden's son by Cole Younger. This is a Colt's Frontier model, 1875, .45 calibre nickel plated, 7½" barrel, serial 70432. Cole used this revolver at Northfield.

Front, left, Captain Wagner's tombstone. Large center stone dedicated to Wagner and 17 Union soldiers who died fighting the guerrillas at Independence, October 23, 1864.

Captain George Todd's grave at Independence, Misouri.

Monument to Quantrill raid victims, Lawrence. *Kansas State Historical Society.*

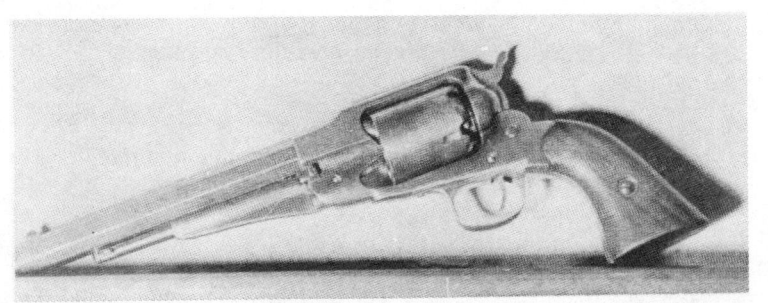

Cole Younger carried this cap and ball percussion Remington revolver during the Civil War.

Massachusetts Street, Lawrence, Kansas, probably 1863. *Kansas State Historical Society.*

"The Ruins of Lawrence" from *Harper's Weekly*, September 19, 1863. *Kansas State Historical Society.*

A Narrow Escape

After the escape from Peabody's cavalry, Cole Younger rested for several days in the home of a friend, Amos Blythe. A report of his whereabouts reached the Federals at Independence, and a force was sent out to capture him. Cole received a warning, and when Quantrill wanted to stage an ambush Cole told him that there was a defile where the road from Independence to Harrisonville ran between two hills. It was called Blue Cut, and this route would be the one the Federals would travel on their way to the Blythe home. It was agreed to ambush the Union soldiers at that spot, but first to warn the elderly Blythe.

The guerrilla band rode fast to the wooded spot known as Blue Cut and hid in the brushy growth near the road. Anxiously they lay in wait for the Union troops for most of that spring afternoon. At last, impatient, Quantrill feared that the plan had miscarried. He sent his most able lieutenant, Cole Younger, to investigate.

When Cole was several miles from Blue Cut, an excited Negro named Mose ran toward him, arms waving wildly, eyes rolling in his ashen face. At first the darky was so overcome with fright and emotion that he jabbered incoherently. Cole patiently waited to hear what had happened, and finally learned that the Union soldiers had been to "Massa Blythe's house, an' dey done kill de po' chile."

Mose told how the Federals had descended in force on the Blythe house and demanded to be told the whereabouts of the elderly owner of the place. Several of the soldiers took Blythe's twelve-year-old son into the barn and threatened to hang him unless he told them the hiding place of his father and Quantrill. But the little lad bravely refused and, jerking away from the men, raced to the house, got an old revolver, and made a dash for the adjacent woods. The soldiers spied the running boy, fired at him, and the bullets struck him in the back. Even though seriously wounded, the boy determined to die fighting. He pulled the trigger of the ancient gun twice and killed two of the soldiers. Then, before he could finish whispering the little prayer that was on his lips, a volley was fired at him and he fell dead, his slim young body pierced by seventeen bullets.

Cole Younger's eyes flashed, his brow knitted, and his jaw set while he listened to old Mose tell of this cowardly crime of the Federals. Rushing to an elevated place on the road, he made a quick survey and, to his grim delight, saw the troops coming from the south. Apparently they had taken a roundabout route to the Blythe home and thus had bypassed Blue Cut. Now they were advancing on the narrow road which led to the cut. Cole dashed back to where Quantrill waited and told him what had happened. Every man of the guerrillas vowed to slay as many soldiers as possible, and the byword was "Remember young Blythe!"

Without the slightest thought of pending disaster, the Union soldiers, in high fettle on such a beautiful afternoon, whistled and sang as they rode on their way back to their quarters in town. They chatted and laughed, the murder of the boy entirely forgotten. Into the defile they rode their horses. All of a sudden their gay laughter was silenced by a burst of gunfire that dealt out death and painful wounds to them. Killing and wild confusion reigned in that cut in the timber-lined lane. Men and horses fell in mad disorder in an effort to get out of that deathtrap. When the firing finally ceased, twenty-eight of the force of thirty lay sprawled in death. The Blythe lad had been avenged!

And from their sheltered position in the woods, not a single guerrilla had been hit by a Federal bullet. They were jubilant over their victory. Quantrill selected a remote spot on the banks of Indian Creek, in Jackson County, where he and his followers retreated for food and rest.

It would be difficult to quote all the ravings of the surprised and chagrined Federal officers, who never had dreamed such a

A NARROW ESCAPE

defeat by the guerrillas possible. And the taunts of the local people made life more miserable for them. Captain E. Neugent and Captain Irvin Walley of the Enrolled Missouri Militia took soldiers and searched hills and vales in an all-out effort to locate the hideout of the cunning Quantrill and his band. When they finally learned of the hidden retreat in the woods near Indian Creek, Union soldiers prepared to exterminate the foxy guerrillas.

Open ground lay all around the timbered area in which Quantrill was entrenched, and the soldiers thought they would have an easy task. They considered their plan something of a picnic; with bands playing and banners waving, the large body of soldiers marched out of the town of Independence, taking along two pieces of artillery—all for a handful of determined men!

The Federal officers had the element of surprise in their favor. It was one time when Quantrill's friends among the civilians had no time to warn him of the advance of the enemy. All the exits out of Independence were carefully guarded, and no one was permitted to leave the town until after the departure of the troops. The Federals were able to place their two cannon where they would command the road leading into the thicket; their cavalry guarded the open country all along the other side of the wooded area.

It was a desperate situation for the guerrillas, who may have begun to wonder why they had picked such a quiet place for a hideout. Without an instant's warning, a terriffic barrage was laid down by the two cannon, and the scream of the shells was the first warning Quantrill had of the presence of the Union troops.

As usual in a situation of extreme peril, Quantrill sought Younger's advice. A quick sortie from the woods would bring the entire force down upon them; to remain in hiding would mean inevitable destruction from the continued fire of the cannon as well as small arms. Cole told his chief that there was a stock farm within Federal lines, and he suggested the large number of animals might be stampeded into the ranks of the soldiers.

"In the confusion," Cole explained, "when those damn Yankees are trying to keep themselves from being trampled to death, we could make our escape. It seems to be our only chance."

Quantrill was elated. He recognized that the stampeding cattle would seem to have been frightened by the roar of the cannon and gunfire.

"As you say, Cole, it is our only chance, and we will take it," Quantrill concluded.

It was a risky chance at best, but still a chance that the guerrilla band might stay alive. They sat tight a little while, until the then gathering dusk darkened into night. When the bombardment ceased, the men hidden in the woods breathed a sigh of relief. Apparently the soldiers were planning on making a grand assault the next morning. It was now or never, for well Quantrill knew they would stand no chance of survival once the infantry stormed their citadel.

The difficult and dangerous mission of stealing through the Federal lines was entrusted to those two skilled woodsmen, Cole Younger and Jim Haller. They got through safely, and, on reaching the cattle, stampeded them. This was easy, because the animals were already restless and fearful at the way the roar of the cannon had disrupted their peaceful pastures. They now rushed madly, terrorized and bellowing, toward the Union lines.

The sleeping soldiers were awakened by the noise and, when they realized farm animals were stampeding from the opposite direction from their quarry, they were not at all suspicious of any trick. They simply made way for the flying hoofs of the cattle, horses, and mules. Under the cover of the night and this diversion, Quantrill and his men ran trailing in the wake of the animals. Amid the bawling and bellowing, the clouds of thick dust and confusion, the fleeing guerrillas were not seen by the soldiers. In single file the guerrillas crawled past the sentries and made their way to freedom and safety. They all heartily agreed later that it had been their tightest spot.

One of the men casually remarked that it would have been a good joke on the "damn Yankees" if they had captured the two cannon. This was such a good idea that Quantrill considered it, and the more he thought about it the better he liked it. Such a capture certainly would eclipse all the former exploits of the small band, if it could be accomplished under the very noses of at least one hundred Unionists.

Cole offered to reconnoiter to determine the number of soldiers guarding the cannon and if possible to find the placements of the large forces of infantry. For more than an hour he scouted around the Federal camp. He learned that the cavalry had been dismounted in apparent readiness to assist the foot soldiers in the attack on the wooded spot where they believed Quantrill to be still hiding. Cole also noticed that only a very small group guarded the prized brass cannon. Quickly he returned to relay this information to his chief. It was decided to attack the cannon position at break of day.

Dawn's first faint light was just breaking over the eastern horizon when a large detachment of cavalry was seen approaching from the east. Quantrill thought this might be a scouting party for the Confederate Army; but Cole Younger did not think so. The approaching horsemen also caused alarm in the Union encampment, for they evidently believed the riders to be Confederates.

Quantrill saw that this was the opportune moment to strike, and he did so. A furious charge was made on the men guarding the cannon, and those who were not killed fled in complete disorder, so great was their surprise. Quickly George Todd, an experienced artilleryman, opened fire on the Federals with their own cannon. The horses of the soldiers stampeded, and that, together with the cannon fire, caused the approaching horsemen to turn about and go galloping away from the place. It was later found that the fleeing men were Jayhawkers under Jennison who would have been pleased to join the Federals fighting Quantrill. Imagine the delight of Quantrill and his group at having made such a wonderful coup! Besides, imagine the rage and embarrassment of the Jayhawkers and the Unionists! Had they only known each other's identity, the curtain on Quantrill's life and the lives of his men would have fallen that day.

Quantrill's men put the two cannon out of commission and then rolled them into the stream for they had no use for heavy artillery in their hit-and-run tactics.

At first, news of this disastrous defeat of the Federal troops by a mere handful of guerrillas was not believed by the top officers in Kansas City. But when it was confirmed they realized how ridiculous they looked. They decided to take dramatic measures to dispose of Quantrill's roving band without delay. Jennison and his organization of cutthroats received orders to report to Union Headquarters in Kansas City. There they were given instructions to loot, destroy, burn, and maim—anything to make the Missourians quaver at the sight of Union men, for the Missourians had of course been supporting Quantrill.

This order was like turning a weasel loose in a brooder of chicks. Homes were looted of food and valuables and then the torch was applied; men were killed, women ravaged, innocent children tortured and maimed. All suffered alike, rich and poor. No pro-slavery family or individual was spared. Although the soldiers of the Union Army did not ride with these raiders, the people knew that Jennison and his outlaws were sanctioned in their vile work by the Union leaders.

Blue Cut Again

By this time Quantrill's riders had swelled to more than a hundred in number. They were angry men, yearning to wreak vengeance on the Kansas Redlegs and Jayhawkers. A council of war was held in Quantrill's camp, and several companies were formed under Lieutenants Younger and Haller, with George Todd assisting. By breaking into four groups, with Quantrill himself leading the fourth, they hoped they would be able to cope with the movements of Jennison and his raiders and to destroy many of them.

Numerous informers came to Quantrill with news of the whereabouts and movements of Jennison, and Quantrill or one of his groups was there to meet them at every turn. Jennison and his men were hated and feared; on the other hand, Quantrill and his guerrillas were received everywhere with open arms, fed and clothed, and given fresh mounts by the Southern sympathizers. The vast majority of Missourians were pro-slavery in feeling, and it was their wish to destroy or have destroyed all those who expressed Union ideals or uttered anything against Quantrill and his followers.

In June, three guerrillas were ambushed by a band of Federal soldiers, two of them killed and the other taken into Independence as prisoner. Quantrill was furious, and more so several days later when he learned that his man was to be hanged publicly in the town square. He realized that if he could capture a number of soldiers he could hold them as hostages and thus be able to dicker with the commander for an exchange of prisoners.

Haller's mother lived in Independence at the time, and it was agreed that he should go into town in disguise to learn the location of the pickets. This would enable the guerrillas to sweep silently down in the night and take several of them. Haller found out that several detachments of pickets were stationed at each end of the town, one near an old mill and one next to an abandoned wagon factory. This was perturbing news. It meant that while they were attacking one group the other would rally and come to their fellows' aid. So it was suggested that Cole Younger should distract the attention of the pickets at the old wagon factory building, while Haller would try to capture those at the mill.

But Cole was unwilling to be outdone. He, too, wanted to bring in some prisoners. Silently and quickly he descended upon the unsuspecting soldiers at the wagon factory, and amid a shower of bullets and a bedlam of wild yells he carried off five of the Union men.

While Cole's group was busy there, Haller and his men struck at the mill. Their attack was such a complete surprise that they were able to get away with more than twenty prisoners. Quantrill sent word to the commander at Independence that if he wanted his soldiers back he would have to release the guerrilla held in jail and all the aged folk he had taken prisoners, as well as to give his word not to molest them further. The commandant could do nothing but abide by Quantrill's proposition. So the exchange of prisoners was quickly effected.

Not long after this affair, Cole Younger visited the home of his grandmother, Mrs. Fristoe. It was a trap, for the house was surrounded by soldiers. When he was taking his leave, he was confronted by Captain Charles Younger* of the United States Militia. This captain was Cole's cousin, and therefore when he announced that he had come to arrest him Cole thought he was joking. When the captain assured him that he was in deadly earnest, Cole drew his revolver and killed his cousin

---

*Some writers have claimed there were no Youngers from Missouri in the Federal forces in that state. As late as May 24, 1865, by order of General Fisk in his dispatch to Colonel Denny at Glasgow, Mo., another Captain Younger was ordered to Richmond, Ray County, to hunt the bushwhackers.

instantly by shooting him in the face. In the confusion, Cole made his escape in the darkness, by running into the wooded tract close by his grandmother's home.

As was their custom, the Federals again took up their scythe for a sweep of destruction in retaliation for the capture of the pickets in Independence and for the forced release of the prisoners, as well as for the killing of Captain Charles Younger by his guerrilla kinsman.

However, this latest campaign was cut short by the Union's Major J. Linden, the new Commander at Harrisonville who was in charge of the Seventh Volunteer Missouri Cavalry. The major's mode of warfare was an honorable one, and he did not approve of the atrocities that had been permitted by the former officer in charge. But Neugent and Walley were determined to carry on their own sort of fighting, and incessantly they harassed the major until he could no longer endure it. He resigned his command at Harrisonville.

During the lull imposed by Major Linden, the guerrillas had been busy keeping the soldiers on the run and causing consternation in their ranks. It was a favorite trick of Quantrill's to send Cole Younger with several men close to the camps of the Federal forces, to taunt them. Invariably, the soldiers pursued Younger—right into an ambush of waiting guerrillas who exterminated them. It was common gossip that Cole Younger bore a charmed life; and eventually the Union soldiers refrained from giving chase when they saw that guerrilla.

In one attack on a Federal convoy, Quantrill was shocked to see that his men had obtained five sacks of United States mail. This was not to his liking or approval, for he had no cause to rob the mails and did not want to do so. Yet he was curious to know what effect this act on the part of some of his men would have on future mail runs. He learned that a wagon train carrying mail was leaving Harrisonville, en route to Independence under heavy escort of Neugent's Jayhawkers. The route ran through the deep defile called Blue Cut, where Union soldiers had previously met disaster.

A runner informed Cole Younger that Captain Long was in

charge of the group. Cole remarked that Long had always been a good friend of the Youngers and that he regretted Long's presence there that day. Cole went so far as to give his fellow guerrillas a description of Captain Long of the Union Army, urging them not to fire in his direction.

The Union soldiers joked about what had happened at the Cut some time before, feeling safe on this occasion since they had been assured that Quantrill had left that part of the country to go south.

When the mail wagons and the Union soldiers entered the Cut, they were surprised by guerrillas who called on them to surrender. They refused, and the Quantrill men opened fire, shooting many of them down, dead or wounded. The guerrillas were closing in on the soldiers when Captain Long rode at them, saber swinging. Calmly, Cole Younger shot his horse from under him, pinning him to the ground and injuring his leg, thus deliberately saving Long's life. The fight was soon over, and Cole spoke in a friendly manner to Long and permitted him to go in peace with his wounded men.

Much to Younger's surprise, his act in sparing the life of Captain Long infuriated the Federals all the more. To have a large number of prisoners taken by the lawless guerrillas and treated as prisoners of war was intolerable. The Federal Commander in Jackson County let it be known that he was determined to exterminate the guerrillas at all costs; and every available man was thrown into a giant search of the entire countryside. More than two thousand of the Blue Coats began searching hills and vales for Quantrill's gang.

Quantrill decided it was time to strike in another county and made plans for an attack on the town of Harrisonville, Missouri, in Cass County. They were only one mile from that county seat when a large detachment of Federal soldiers came into view and gave them chase. They retired to a neighboring town, where they were disappointed at not finding any soldiers there. However, they soon saw another large body of soldiers approaching the town—apparently about one thousand men. Aware that it would be suicidal for his men to try to cope with such a large force, Quantrill gave the order to retreat into the Blue Hills, from which vantage point in that timbered terrain they could send out parties to harass the Federals from the rear. But again they were seen.

Quickly the band of seventy-five, led by Quantrill, raced over the road to Walnut Creek, in Jackson County. Once over the stream, they took to the dense woods, throwing the pursuing Federals off their trail. Their respite, however, was brief. Hardly had they reined up their mounts to rest, when a sentry rushed into camp with the news that about two hundred soldiers were approaching. The lay of the land was in favor of the guerrillas, who fell back into a large area of timber flanked on two sides by steep hills. They worked desperately, felling trees to close the entrance to their retreat, and they made an effective barricade with room for only one horse and one rider to pass through.

Cole Younger, always at the fore in Quantrill's band, went to a small house nearby and persuaded the woman of the house to hang blankets and bed quilts across the fence in front of her home. Behind this screen the guerrillas hid and waited for the advance column of Federal soldiers, which numbered fifteen men. When they were close to the fence, the hidden guerrillas stepped from behind the blankets, and the Federal soldiers were met with a withering fire.

At the sight of the slaughter of the entire advance force, the main body of soldiers appeared to be confused. Before they could retreat or attack, they were reinforced by about two hundred men from Butler. By this time, the band of guerrillas had taken their stand behind the improvised barrier, and a steady fire created panic in the ranks of the Federals. Several times a large body of soldiers attacked the barricade, only to be driven back by a fire of pistol, shotgun, and rifle shots.

It was Quantrill's plan to force a break in the Federal lines by making a sortie; but this was a failure. In the distance, another line of blue-coated cavalry was approaching. More than a thousand cavalrymen were now in the field, and to make a thrust at such a formidable force would mean only one thing—the extermination of the entire guerrilla band.

Seven times the Federals attacked the fort, and each time the deadly fire of shotguns at close range was too much for them. Both Quantrill and Cole Younger realized that flight was their only hope; and in order to deceive the Federal commanders, they made frantic efforts to strengthen the barricade. The ruse worked. In the dead of the moonless night, the guerrillas stole noiselessly from their place of concealment and reached the hills in safety. To throw off pursuit completely, they broke into singles and disappeared in the dense woods.

Independence and Lone Jack

On August 7, 1862, Quantrill met in council with the Confederate Colonel J. T. Hughes and some of his men. They made a mutual agreement to attack Independence, Missouri, where a strong detachment of the Union troops was quartered. Colonel Hughes was anxious to learn the enemy's weakest points, so Cole Younger volunteered to go into the town in disguise as an old woman, to get this information. His spying escapade was a success, and he returned with the full data of the exact location of the encampments and the munition depots. Colonel Buell, with over six hundred men, was in Independence.

On August 11th the combined forces of Quantrill and Hughes attacked the town. About five hundred soldiers were dislodged and took refuge behind a stone wall out at the edge of town. After hours of steady firing on both sides, finally Cole announced to his friends that he was going to storm the stone wall, and the guerrillas agreed heartily with this decision. A furious battle ensued, with the Federals being driven from their refuge. A withering fire was poured into their ranks. They sustained such heavy loss that the survivors surrendered in a short time.

While this was going on, Quantrill, with a small detachment of men, was attacking the Independence bank building, in which several hundred Federal troops had taken refuge. When Cole joined him he suggested a way to dislodge the Federals. They obtained a large amount of dry straw from behind the bank building, and packed it at the front door, then set fire to it. Smoke and flames filled the building, and the trapped soldiers tried desperately to extinguish the blaze, each time driven back by a hail of bullets. The whole building became ablaze, and Buell surrendered to Colonel Hughes and Quantrill. The hundreds of prisoners were released on parole, granted right there on the field. In this fight 26 of the Union men had been killed, 30 wounded, and 256 were missing. No Confederate record can be found, and no report on the losses under Hughes' command seems to have been made; but Quantrill's command listed eleven guerrillas slain.

The Battle of Lone Jack, Missouri, was fought only five days later, on August 16, 1862. Major Emory L. Foster, stationed at Lexington as commander of the Union forces there, rode out with a contingent to avenge Independence and to capture Quantrill. In the meantime, the guerrillas had been reinforced by the troops of the Confederate Colonel Francis M. Cockrell, who had come to Missouri to enlist recruits for the Confederate Army. Foster had in his command almost a thousand men and two pieces of Rabb's Indiana Battery. He was unaware of Cockrell's presence and did not realize it until he stumbled upon his forces at Lone Jack.

Colonel Cockrell, later a United States Senator, while recruiting had planned a meeting with Colonels Upton Hays, Tracy, Jackman, and Rathburn for a surprise attack on Kansas City, Missouri. That city was spared a terrible fight only by the attack of Foster's men at Lone Jack. The residents of Lone Jack were Confederate in sympathy, and Major Foster of the Union Army ordered the Indiana Battery to open up on the little town. Cockrell withdrew to the west, and Colonel John T. Coffee to the south, thus cutting the Confederate command in two. Colonel Hays arrived with his command and agreed to attack Foster in the morning.

The battle began at daylight on the 16th, an accidental shot giving Foster the alarm. For five hours furious fighting raged, most of it across the road from the small town of Lone Jack. The Indiana Battery was charged by Jackman and his men, who captured the two cannon. Shortly afterward, Major Foster led a gallant charge against Jackman and recaptured the big guns. The Confederate forces were almost out of ammunition.

INDEPENDENCE AND LONE JACK

Had Foster known that and had he pressed the attack, he would have destroyed the entire command.

Cole Younger it was who rushed to the wagons and calmly distributed ammunition among the soldiers at the front lines. Quantrill was not in this battle, although his squads under Gregg and Jarrette came up shortly after the fighting stopped and chased the Federals back toward Lexington.

The Union forces were put to rout, and Cole Younger and his men again disbanded, with instructions to meet Quantrill as soon as possible wherever they could. People to this day still talk of the terrible fight at Lone Jack; and many youngsters in that part of the state of Missouri still think it was the largest battle of the Civil War. The official records show hat the Union losses were 43 killed, 54 wounded, 73 missing; the Confederates had 118 killed and wounded.

That year, 1862, Quantrill led his band on numerous raids into Kansas and improved his reputation as a fearless leader. In October he made a raid on Olathe, Kansas, with about one hundred fifty men. He kept the citizens under guard in the public square while his men carried off whatever they wanted in the way of horses and goods. During this raid they killed only one man.

This Olathe raid was so successful and profitable that soon similar raids were made at Spring Hill, Aubrey, and other Kansas towns. For instance, at Shawnee, Kansas, Quantrill found and captured nearly a hundred untrained militia without firing a single shot, and he paroled them.

Various citizens of Clarke, Lewis, and Shelby Counties, in a desperate attempt to get protection from these continuously threatening raids, addressed President Lincoln on the seriousness of the situation:

Northern Missouri, January 1, 1863.
His Excellency Abraham Lincoln,
President of the United States:
Your memorialists, loyal citizens of the United States and of the State of Missouri, respectfully represent that, since the outbreak of

the present rebellion, Northern Missouri, in common with the southern part of the State, has been infested by hordes of lawless depredators, popularly known as guerrillas, though styling themselves "Confederate soldiers," led by desperate and unprincipled men, having not even the form of official commissions from the authorities of the so-called Confederate States, and whose modes of warfare have been only those resorted to and practiced by highway robbers, thieves, murderers, and assassins. Not having from any source a recognition as belligerents, they have, nevertheless, not scrupled to wage relentless war against the Government of the United States and of the State of Missouri, and against the peace, safety, and happiness of the loyal citizens of this State. In thus doing, they have causelessly murdered noncombatants by hanging, by shooting, by cutting their throats, and by divers other cruel, inhuman, and outrageous methods. They have fired into railroad trains, killing and maiming soldiers and citizens, and placing in imminent peril the lives of women and children. They have burned and destroyed railroad bridges, thereby causing trains filled with noncombatants to be precipitated into streams, killing, drowning, and wounding many persons, including women and children. They have, in the darkness of night, summoned citizens to the doors of their dwellings and there shot them dead. They have deliberately, and without provocation, fired into dwellings, placing in extreme jeopardy the lives of innocent and helpless persons therein. They have abducted citizens from their dwellings and families and murdered them secretly, and by methods unknown to the community at large. They have practiced inhuman and diabolical cruelties upon prisoners in their hands by brutally whipping and hanging them until nearly dead. And all this has been done for no other reason than that the parties thus murdered and outraged were, and had been, true and faithful in their allegiance to the United States. More than this, they have robbed the loyal citizens of Northern Missouri of hundreds of thousands of dollars' worth of property, taking in numerous instances the only horse from a needy and dependent family. They have stripped thousands of families of clothing, money, grain, cattle, wagons, arms, and ammunition, and, in short, of everything which their cupidity could lead them to covet or their wants to desire. Nor have these operations been confined to a few or remote localities. Every county, every community, has thus been scourged, until scarcely a loyal family has remained untouched. Thus these desperadoes desolated the whole land, establishing a reign of terror. Under this scourge many loyal citizens have fled from the State to preserve their lives; many have been forced to abandon their families and take refuge in the Federal army, and for weeks and months thousands have been nightly driven to the woods and fields to find shelter from the fury of these prowling fiends.

Your Excellency will not, however, understand that during all this time the United States and State Governments have been inactive in their efforts to crush out rebellion in this section of the State. Many thousand troops have occupied and held the various important points in Northern Missouri, and at no time have these guerrillas been able to withstand, in open conflict, by any combination of their forces, the regularly organized troops of the Government. But the character of their warfare and their intimacy with the topography of the country have been such that eighteen months' experience has demonstrated that organized troops, in however large bodies, simply holding isolated points, with ample power to control any given point, but governed only by the rules and methods of ordinary and regular warfare, could not check the outrages referred to, nor assure peace and safety to the loyal people. Experience long since convinced the military authorities of this department that something more was necessary than the mere occupancy of the country by Federal troops and the dispersion of aggregated bands of marauders. Hence the orders of Generals Halleck and Schofield, the point of which was that all guerrillas taken in arms should be shot. Had those orders in every instance been strictly carried out, it cannot be doubted that the effect would have been most happy. But too many such persons fell into the hands of our military authorities who lacked the nerve to administer the required penalty. The result was thousands of these desperadoes were released on parole and bond; the country was again overrun by them, and their reiterated acts of brigandism were none the less violent or atrocious that they involved the additional crime of perjury. Oaths and bonds imposed no restraint upon such persons, whose demoniac passions now burned with a new and doubly heated flame. . . .

In the summer of 1863 the raids were more numerous, as well as bolder and more arrogant. The entire region along the Kansas-Missouri border was kept in a continual state of confusion and dread. Every night, lights against the sky showed that some poor family's house was going up in flames set by Quantrill's gang. Men on the farms dared not remain in their homes at night but slept in the cornfields and the wooded areas. The depredations seldom extended for more than ten or fifteen miles from the Missouri line, since experience had made Quantrill cautious.

In Lafayette County, Missouri, there lived a family by the name of Fickle, whose daughter Annie is credited with having made the black flag for Quantrill. She was always loud in her praise of the Southern cause and vociferous in her condemnation of the North. Naturally, her outspoken attitude caused her parents much concern and trouble with the Enrolled Missouri Militia which scoured the state for Quantrill and people with Southern leanings. One evening a member of Quantrill's guerrillas was arrested at the Fickle home, and the soldiers took along Miss Annie Fickle also because she put up a fight, kicking and biting the soldiers, clawing them with her fingernails. She was locked up in the jail at Lexington, Missouri, where her guerrilla lover was incarcerated too.

A friend of Annie's, believed to have been George Shepherd, resolved that she should be rescued or released via a prisoner exchange agreement. He knew that she had a cousin who was a Federal officer. Shepherd went to see Annie at the jail, and through her he arranged a meeting with her cousin. He agreed to pay $500 for Annie's release and the release of the captured guerrilla.

Shepherd saw no reason to distrust the officer, whom he met at the agreed time. Together they rode off to take the money to the go-between at the jail. Near a turn in the road, along which ran a high stone fence and deep underbrush, a squad of Federal soldiers rose from concealment and fired at Shepherd. The volley killed his horse, but he managed to draw his revolver and kill Annie's treacherous cousin and then to leap quickly

INDEPENDENCE AND LONE JACK

behind the fence. He raced along the length of the stone wall until he outdistanced the pursuing soldiers. In the blackness of the night the Federals were unable to locate their quarry, and he escaped, miraculously, unharmed.

The guerrilla arrested at the Fickle home was shot by the order of Colonel Blunt, who had previously issued the proclamation that all persons arrested in Jackson County for bearing arms against the Union would be put to death as guerrillas and not treated as prisoners of war. This was no doubt meant to put fear into the minds of any young men who had been harboring the thought of joining Quantrill's band. In any event, no record exists of any more arrests on that account.

The Sacking of Lawrence

In the autumn of 1854 a few families of settlers from New England had come to Kansas Territory and named their new home Lawrence in honor of Amos Lawrence, their leader. The population greatly increased, due to the continuous arrival of Northerners. It was not long before the crude little log cabins gave way to buildings of brick and frame and stone, and the town's growing prosperity aroused the envy of the pro-slavery elements in the Territory. It therefore was the center of the attack by those abettors of slavery in what was known as the Wakarusa War.

To fortify the town, the local citizens erected circular earthworks around it, to a height of about seven feet. These earthworks were connected with long lines of entrenchments and rifle pits. The men of the town were daily drilled by Jim Lane and Charles Robinson (first Governor of Kansas), who also set an around-the-clock guard. The end of the Wakarusa War came in December of 1855; yet most of the men of Lawrence still carried their weapons of defense, always vigilant of approaching danger, because rumors were still heard that Missourians were planning to invade Kansas for the sole purpose of wiping out Lawrence. Their rebel battle cry was, "Wipe out Lawrence! Win Kansas for Slavery—even if we have to wade in blood to our knees!"

In the spring of 1856 mobs of ruffians arrived. Alabama had sent a band of fighters under Colonel Buford; Colonel Titus and a band came from Florida; South Carolina sent Colonel Wilkes with several companies to assist in the fight of winning Kansas Territory for slavery. The President of the United States placed Federal troops at the command of Territorial Governor Wilson Shannon, and Chief Justice Samuel D. Le-

THE SACKING OF LAWRENCE

compte of Douglas County, Kansas, declared openly that all those who resisted the laws would be found guilty of treason.

That infamous character, Sheriff Samuel J. Jones, now came into the picture. He was called the "bogus" sheriff of Douglas County because he had been appointed by the bogus Shawnee Legislature which was repudiated when the constitution was framed at the Topeka Convention on October 23, 1855. This constiution was smothered in the United States Senate after having passed the House, and the officers never took their seats. Nevertheless, the movement served as a bond among the free-state men, and it was their rallying point for two years.

Jones arrested all those he pleased and saw to it that the grand jury declared as nuisances the Free State Hotel and the two newspapers *Herald of Freedom* and the *Kansas Free-State*. Free-staters were molested and killed on the roads and highways, or publicly robbed, with not a soul daring to do anything about the outrages. While this was going on, a large army of the pro-slavery element was daily increasing in numbers and strength to the right and left of Lawrence, all of them loudly boasting that the force had been sent by Providence to destroy the traitorous city and its abolitionist inhabitants.

The night of May 20, 1856, Colonel Buford's troops were encamped a few miles southeast of the doomed town. To the west, about ten miles away, were the armed companies of Colonels Wilkes and Titus. The latter was reinforced by General David R. Atchison with his famous riflemen and two pieces of heavy artillery. Later that night more reinforcements came in the form of Captain Dunn and General Clark's companies and those of General B. F. Stringfellow. Buford's forces formed the lower division of the invading army, the others forming the upper division.

These forces actually were not under the leadership of any military official, but under the direct orders of United States Marshal I. B. Donelson, who considered the entire force as his means to "assist him in the execution of his official duties." His deputy, Mr. H. Fain, entered Lawrence during the early morning hours of May 21st and tried to provoke incidents that would give him an excuse for arresting the citizens. However, they acted wisely and cooperated with the deputy marshal in his making of several token arrests. The marshal then saw that his plan to attack the town was fruitless, so he dismissed his troops, stating that he had no further need of them. On second thought he turned the men over to Sheriff Jones, who seemed to have some business to attend to in Lawrence.

That same afternoon, Jones with twenty-five men rode up to the Free-State Hotel and demanded that General Samuel C. Pomeroy surrender all weapons. He declared that if his order was not complied with within five minutes, the troops would shell the town. Pomeroy had only a few small arms and one howitzer which was not private property, and this was turned over to Sheriff Jones. Jones then advised the people that he would have to carry out the orders of the Douglas County District Court to destroy the newspapers named as nuisances. The presses of these papers were demolished and the pieces thrown into the Kaw River. The soldiers carried out all the furniture and other contents of the buildings and dumped them into the street and burned them.

By this time four cannon had been brought up in front of the Eldridge House by General Atchison, and he ordered his men to fire away at the hotel. Their aim was so devastating that the building burst into flames and was quickly burned to the ground.

At the first roar of the cannons the women and children of Lawrence began to flee the town. Their plight was pitiful, for they didn't know where to go nor which way to turn. Their men stood by, offering no resistance to such an overwhelming force, and had helplessly to watch their homes and places of business looted and destroyed. All afternoon this plundering and destruction went on, but, strange to say, there was no killing. Not one human life was lost, even though those reckless men of pro-slavery sentiments were crazed with drink and wild with lust for plunder.

The Free-State men acted wisely in submitting while they were so helpless and in refraining from later violence against

THE SACKING OF LAWRENCE

their enemies. But after it was all over, driven to desperation, they organized bands of roving guerrillas in an effort to prevent another such disaster.

But perhaps the town of Lawrence, Kansas, was under an evil sign, for there was even worse suffering in store for its peaceable citizens. The never-to-be-forgotten sacking took place on August 21, 1863.

Even the sultry late-summer breeze seemed to whisper cautiously that black night of August 19th when a band of rough and desperate-looking men gathered near the Blackwater River a few miles from Columbus, in Johnson County, Missouri. The cunning and vicious guerrilla chief, William Clarke Quantrill, had assembled his men at the Pardee home earlier in the evening and from there they had ridden over to Lone Jack in Jackson County. The men sensed that something big was in the making and, as time proved, they were right.

Quantrill divulged that he had planned a raid on the town of Lawrence, the home of his archenemy, General (Senator) James Lane. He had planted a spy in Lawrence some weeks before, and tonight they could all hear a report of what had been learned.

"All right, Fletch Taylor," Quantrill said, nodding to one of his guerrillas. "Give it to us now."

Taylor told how he had gone into Lawrence disguised as a horse trader with plenty of money. It had been easy for him to get all the information he wanted, for he had stayed at the Eldridge House, had sat at the same table and eaten his meals with the hated General Lane. Taylor said the city was weakly garrisoned and that the Union camp just across the river was meager. Now was the perfect time to strike, because the thought of Quantrill and his raiders was far from the people's minds. They felt secure because the Union troops were near.

Lawrence had been rebuilt since its earlier catastrophes and it was a beautiful town, known to be the most sightly in the State of Kansas. Having been founded by Amos Lawrence in 1854, it had wide and clean streets lined with trees, many fine stores, neat and comfortable houses. Its population of twelve hundred was prosperous and happy. It was a bustling recruiting center for the Union Army, and therefore it was easy for Quantrill and his gang of outlaws to come riding into town with Stars and Stripes flying at the head of their column to avert suspicion.

At the secret rendezvous on the bank of the Blackwater River that hot night in August, 1863, Quantrill listened to the report and said, "Men, you have heard what Fletch Taylor says. But remember, all of you, taking Lawrence is a big venture—one of the biggest we've ever tackled. It will not be any child's play. We will be harassed all the way, there and back—so we must decide, knowing all this. Anderson"—Quantrill's keen eyes turned to Bloody Bill—"What do you say?"

"I say let's sack the damn town and kill every male thing there!" was Anderson's firm reply.

"Todd?"

"Lawrence it is, regardless of the cost!"

"Gregg?"

"Lawrence is the home of Jim Lane, isn't it? That's enough for me. I say 'Lawrence or death!' "

"Shepherd?"

"I say it's about time we wiped that nigger-lovin' town off the map."

"Jarrette?"

"Burn Lawrence to the ground, just like Lane did Osceola."

"Maddox?"

"Sack Lawrence! Destruction and death to everybody there!"

"Yeager?"

"Lawrence or hell! Let's be quick about it too."

It was unanimous. The men Quantrill had asked were those who had sworn revenge against anything Federal for the rest of their lives. Such men did most of the killing; they worked methodically, not spasmodically as some of the others did.

Quantrill supplied them all with maps of Lawrence, with all the objectionable houses marked for destruction.

It was agreed that they would attack Lawrence the following day, the 20th, but as it turned out the raid actually did not

THE SACKING OF LAWRENCE 121

occur until August 21st. In some mysterious way the rumor had gotten out many weeks earlier that it was Quantrill's intention to raid Lawrence and slaughter the citizens and burn the town. So guards had been stationed at all roads leading into town. When nothing happened for about three months, the people laughed at their own fears. Therefore, when Quantrill struck he found no guards and the town asleep to its danger.

The band rode forth from Lone Jack toward the Kansas Border. There were three hundred of them; one hundred fifty of Quantrill's own men and the same number under Confederate Colonel Holt, who had been detailed there by General Sterling Price. Possibly Price did not know Quantrill's intention, although some people later claimed that Holt had chosen to ride along especially because he owed General Lane a debt of long standing.

At five o'clock that evening, the raiders crossed over the border into Kansas, in plain sight of a Federal command under Captain J. A. Pike, whose force was much too small to invite a clash. Of course Captain Pike hastened into the town of Aubrey and sent word to Kansas City about the guerrilla movement. Why he did not warn Lawrence remains a mystery.

At eleven that night the guerrillas passed Gardner, Kansas, on the old Santa Fe Trail. There they burned a few houses and killed several men. Even after this, word failed to reach Lawrence of Quantrill's advance.

At three in the morning Quantrill passed through Hesper, and here he forced a young lad to lead the band to Lawrence, since the night was pitch-black and the raiders were not familiar with the lay of the land. Quantrill kept the boy with him throughout the raid, then released him and sent him home. Near Captain's Creek one daring Kansan made a desperate effort to give the alarm in Lawrence; but his fast-galloping horse fell and was killed. The name of this Kansas Paul Revere should have been preserved, but it is not recorded.

In the first faint light of dawn, Quantrill and his band entered Franklin, four miles east of Lawrence. A few persons who were up at that early hour saw the men ride through but never dreamed they were any but Federal soldiers. When they were two miles from their destination, the guerrillas passed the farm of the Reverend Snyder. They rode into the minister's barnyard and killed him. His name was on the hate list because he was a Union officer of colored troops.

One mile out of the doomed town, they came upon Hoffman Collamore, the young son of Lawrence's Mayor Collamore. The boy was out hunting game, and he supposed the body of horsemen were Federal troops on the march. When he was asked where he was going by one of the mounted men, Hoffman told him he was out early hunting. Without any warning some of the guerrillas began firing at him. He turned and ran into a field but was brought down by a volley of gunfire. He had the presence of mind to lie perfectly still on the ground, to make the murderous raiders think he was dead. After they had ridden on, he crawled to a house where he got help, having suffered a severe thigh wound.

The weak eyes of another man, Joe Savage, saved his life that early August morning. Two of the guerrillas knocked on his door, meaning to kill anyone inside. Unable to find his eyeglasses, Savage did not open the door right away; when he did finally open it, his visitors were gone. He too figured they were Union soldiers.

So quiet and unsuspecting was Lawrence, that Quantrill sent two scouts into the town to look things over. They rode down the main street and were seen by the few citizens who were up and about, but no slightest suspicion was excited. The two men went back to the waiting guerrillas to report that all was well and that the attack should commence at once.

Across the Kansas River there were about four hundred Union soldiers, but on the Lawrence side there were no more than seventy. Quantrill's men guarded the river front and took possession of the ferry, thus making sure that the troops could not cross the river. The soldiers on the Lawrence side were slaughtered as they slept, probably never knowing what struck them.

THE SACKING OF LAWRENCE

However, this diversion did not check the speed of the general advance. A few of the guerrillas turned aside to pursue some of the fleeing soldiers, but the main body swept on down Rhode Island Street.

Suddenly Quantrill yelled, "On to the hotel! Quick!"

Along Massachusetts Street tore the raiders, on toward the Eldridge House. Each horse and rider seemed to be one as the guerrillas went racing by, firing at every moving thing and into every house and building as they went. Men who came out to see what was happening were shot down, left wounded or dying on the wooden sidewalks. Women ran screaming in shock and terror. Those hardened murderers were not avenging Osceola—they were slaughtering Kansans merely because Quantrill wanted it that way. It was his personal revenge he sought in that particular town—because once he had been driven out of it.

Not even among those who ordered the Slaughter of the Innocents, or the barbarian warriors of Attila the Hun, or those under Genghis Khan had there been more merciless and vicious killers than those who spread destruction and desolation that day in Lawrence, Kansas. With demoniac yells the raiders dragged husbands and fathers from their houses and shot them down in the presence of loved ones. Entreaties fell on deaf ears and stony hearts as the death-dealing maniacs ravaged the town. The glare of the rising sun blended horribly with the glare of flames from burning houses that had been marked on the maps. All the stores and business houses along the main street were burned, except one.

In front of the hotel known as the Eldridge House Quantrill reined his horse. The building was silent. The grim guerrilla chieftain hesitated, fearing that the silence was a trap. Suddenly Captain A. R. Banks, Provost Marshal of Kansas, opened a window and displayed a white sheet, signifying surrender. He called out to Quantrill that he would turn the hotel over to him and asked that the people inside it be spared and treated as prisoners of war. Quantrill accepted the surrender. He marched the occupants of the hotel to the corner of Winthrop

Street and told them to take refuge in the City Hotel, where they would be safe.

"I once stayed at the City Hotel, and the Stone family were kind to me," he announced. "Nothing will happen to them or their property while I'm in town."

The torch then was applied to the Eldridge House, and the raiders left it in flames as they rode on, intent on pillage and murder. They spread out in groups of six or eight, taking over each street methodically, house by house. They recognized no code. They were utterly devoid of pity as they killed and destroyed and plundered. The military men and others who knew Quantrill's past record fled in panic and hid wherever they could find a refuge. Later there were rumors that Jesse James was present at the Lawrence massacre, but he was not there. It is true that his brother, Frank James, and Cole Younger were there. Jesse, however, was at that time only a new recruit and Quantrill had refused to let him ride on the dangerous raid. Cole Younger had so far never seen Jesse James.

It is impossible to narrate all the horrors that were perpetrated in Lawrence on that never-to-be-forgotten morning, and the few incidents mentioned here were only a small percentage of the outrages committed. Many were killed. Many others were hiding in houses or barns at the outskirts of the town with no way of knowing what was happening to friends and neighbors. They could, however, see the high-shooting flames and hear the agonized screams.

After the raiders fired the Eldridge House, they went galloping to the Johnson House. There the male occupants were marched across the street and shot without formality. One of them, a man named Hampton, fell to the ground and feigned death; after the raiders rode on, he crawled to safety, although badly wounded. The three Dix brothers were wounded, but they tried to escape by crawling through a rear window. They were discovered in the effort, and two of them were shot and killed; the third got out through the window and hid. The Mayor of Lawrence, George W. Collamore, lived in the western part of town, and there the guerrillas dashed, thinking he might try to organize resistance. Collamore saw them coming and realized there was no safe place to hide in the house. Quickly he thought of a trick that he hoped would work. He and a friend, Pat Keefe, slipped down into the well. The raiders, failing to find him, burned his home to the ground. After the flames had died down and the outlaws had ridden on, to continue their work of destruction, Mrs. Collamore went to the well and called to her husband. There was no response. Captain J. G. Lowe then lowered himself down into the well to see what had happened to the mayor and Pat Keefe. In Captain Lowe's haste he slipped and fell to his death. The mayor and Keefe were already dead, suffocated by the dense smoke from the burning buildings. Mrs. Collamore did not yet know that her young son had already been shot and wounded early that morning on his hunting trip.

Close by the home of the mayor lived Dr. Griswold, with State Senator S. M. Thorpe, Josiah Trask, editor of the *State Journal,* and Harlow Baker, with their wives. The bloodthirsty guerrillas attacked the house, demanding that the occupants surrender. The men inside were armed and were determined not to give up their lives without a fight. More of the citizens of Lawrence might have been armed for protection that black day, had it not been for the mayor's decree that all guns and ammunition should be kept in a central arsenal—and that arsenal had fallen into the hands of Quantrill at the first onslaught.

The leader of one of the raiding bands shouted to those inside Dr. Griswold's residence, "Come out, men! We don't mean to harm you. We want to burn the town, not to kill its people."

Incredibly the four men inside the doctor's house believed this lie. They walked out and permitted the guerrillas to take them prisoners. About one hundred feet from the house they were shot down deliberately, with their four wives looking on in horror. The screaming, weeping women were not allowed to go near the bodies of their husbands. After this shooting the killers returned to the house, plundered it of all the valuables they could carry, then burned the building. Half an hour later, others of the raiding party rode by, saw the bodies lying on the ground, and shot at them again. The women had no way of knowing whether their husbands were dead until after the raiders had left. Dr. Griswold and Mr. Trask were dead. Thorpe died the next day, and Harlow Baker, though wounded, lived to tell of this horrible experience.

One small gang raided the home of Judge Louis Carpenter, whose kind and genial disposition surprised the outlaws and so impressed them that they left without harming him or destroying his home. A later detachment, however, was less inclined to appreciate him. One rider dismounted and chased the judge into his home, firing at him as he ran. Badly wounded, he ran to the cellar and, later, when he went out into his yard he fell mortally wounded. His bride threw herself over him to protect him from the waiting outlaw who had shot him. The brute walked around her, his pistol in his hand, seeking a way to finish the wounded judge. He finally jerked up the girl's arm, thrust the revolver under it, and fired into the head of the helpless man, splashing his brains into her face. The raider then set fire to the Carpenter house, but the Judge's sister-in-law managed to put out the flames.

At the Fitch home, when Mr. Fitch came to the door in response to the loud knocking, he was shot point-blank and fell dead in the doorway while his murderer kept firing bullets into his dead body. His wife, shrieking and hysterical, was forced out of the burning house without being allowed even to take her husband's picture from the wall. Even with shooting and dying going on all around him, the heartles killer noticed the new boots his victim was wearing and knelt down to remove them, then put them on his own feet. While the house was burning, the outbuildings caught fire, and several of the ruffians spied a small United States flag tacked on the wall of a child's playhouse. The sight of the flag seemed to evoke a burst of bitter hatred, for they cursed.

They next entered The Country Store where James Eldridge

and Jim Perine were working as clerks. The intruders demanded the key to the store's iron safe, promising the two men safety if they complied. Given the key, they plundered the safe of all the money, then turned on the young clerks and shot them dead. Men were killed right and left in cold blood. No pity was shown except in very rare cases. Cole Younger, sickened by the carnage, maneuvered to save a few lives that day, and this was remembered in his favor many years afterward.

A man named Burt was slain as he handed all his money to one of the raiders. A Mr. Murphy was shot through the head while another victim drank some water he had brought him. Ellis, a blacksmith, grabbed up his child and hid in a nearby cornfield, and they would have escaped had not the baby begun to cry. When their hiding place was found the father was killed and the baby left in his arms, still crying. One house that was set aflame was the home of a very sick man. He was carried from his bed and put down in the yard at what seemed a safe distance from the burning house. One of the raiders came up to the sick man and shot and killed him in the presence of his wife and children. One horrible deed was surpassed by another as the day of terror dragged on.

Just south of the business district, a Mr. Palmer had a gun repair shop. His building was apart from the others, and a customer was chatting with him. Suddenly the two men became aware that the house was surrounded by the guerrillas who opened fire. Both men were hit and wounded. The building was set afire. While the flames leaped up, the brutes tied the hands of the wounded men together and threw them both into the fire. Several times they made desperate efforts to escape, but each time they were pushed back in.

J. W. Thornton went running out of his house, but he was shot three times—in the hip, through the shoulder, and through the cheek. His would-be murderer cursed: "Damn you, I can kill you another way!" With that, he beat the injured man over the head with his revolver. Mrs. Thornton came rushing out to her husband's defense, and the guerrilla laughed at her as he walked away. Strangely enough, Thornton lived for many years after that, but he was crippled. He did not like to talk of his horrible experience, which he called "a bloody nightmare."

No male citizens—not the young, nor the middle-aged, nor the old—were spared. Even some of the small children were killed. Otis Lonley, a man past sixty, lived a short distance from Lawrence. Two pickets stationed to watch for soldiers paid him a visit and shot him while his poor old wife wept and begged them to spare him.

"He has not committed any crime. He never took part in anything political!" she cried.

"He's a damn Kansas Jayhawker, and that's crime enough," they replied.

It took a number of shots to kill the old man.

The pleadings of the women sometimes saved their houses and other property, seldom the life of a male citizen. George Sargent was slain while his frenzied wife clung to him. The bullet came so close to killing her, too, that for the rest of her life she carried a scar on her neck.

Former Governor of Kansas Charles Robinson saw the entire carnage from beginning to end. He stayed hidden in a large stone barn on his farm, overlooking the town. The raiders went to the farm dwelling and, when they were told that the governor was not at home, they eyed the stout-looking stone barn but kept a healthy distance from it. Perhaps they remembered other stone and brick buildings and wanted no part of Governor Robinson's big rock barn.

It was later said that if the people of Lawrence had received a little warning before the raid and had had time to entrench themselves in some of the stone buildings, with guns and ammunition or even without them, the raid would not have cost so many lives. But such warning had not come. The town had been caught entirely unaware.

It was easy to identify the raiders, for they all wore clothing of a butternut hue. At the butternut-garbed horsemen the soldiers across the river fired Minié balls as soon as they came within range. For that reason a number of buildings within range of the soldiers' rifles were saved from destruction. The guerrillas had come to Lawrence to shoot and kill—not to be shot at.

Those of the men of Lawrence who were not killed had escaped by fleeing into the cornfields and hiding among the tall stalks and weeds. One of the most effective refuges was the large cyclone cellar in the center of the town. It had an entrance almost totally hidden from view, and near it a brave young woman took her stand and directed men and boys who were being chased by the guerrillas. The raiders questioned her, but she insisted she had no knowledge of the missing men. Some were killed before they could reach the storm shelter. One man was saved because when he was shot in the arm he fell in such a position that the body of another victim almost covered him. The pursuing raiders thought both the fallen men were dead and ran past.

District Attorney Samuel A. Riggs had a remarkable escape. Set upon by one of the vilest of the gang, he struck the ruffian's pistol from his hand before he could shoot. Then he ran for his life while his wife grabbed the bridle rein of the guerrilla's horse and clung to it. The horseman rode after Riggs, all the time with Mrs. Riggs clinging to the reins. She held on, while she was dragged around the yard, over a woodpile, and back into the street. When the guerrilla was about to fire another shot Mrs. Riggs jerked violently on the rein and spoiled his aim. By the time he got control of his plunging, frightened mount, the brave lady was safely away. Lucky for her that Quantrill had ordered his men not to shoot any women.

The Reverend H. D. Fisher also had a remarkable escape. The preacher was particularly wanted by the Quantrillians because they knew he served as chaplain of a Kansas regiment doing war service in Missouri. Fisher realized that flight was out of the question, so he hid in the cellar. It was partly excavated, and he climbed up onto a bank under the floor of the house and hid in a drain by the farthest wall. The raiders came down into the cellar searching for him or anyone else who might be hiding there.

"Damn that Yankee preacher!" Fisher heard one of the searchers say.

Another growled, "Yes, damn him. He's got to be somewhere around here. He didn't have time to get away."

"Set the dirty place afire! Kansas wood burns fast!"

"Yes, that ought to flush him out!"

Mrs. Fisher kept putting out the fires the guerrillas set until they became too many. She quickly went through the motions of pouring water here and there, while she aimed so that the water went through the floor and fell upon her hiding husband. When she finally had to flee the burning house, Fisher crawled out a window near the rear door. His clever and loyal wife was there to cover him with a large carpet, and she rolled him up inside it. A neighbor helped Mrs. Fisher drag the rolled carpet out through the back yard and into some weeds and tall shrubbery. All sorts of household furniture and utensils were then piled around the edges of the carpet, and so the Reverend Fisher was protected from the wrath of the raiders.

Young John Speer hid under a sidewalk, but the heat from the burning buildings set the walk on fire and he was forced into the open street. Surrounded by the mounted guerrillas, he gave his name as John Smith, and all unknowingly he saved his life by that. One of the ruffians had some friends named Smith. John had a teen-age brother who had been sleeping in the office of a local newspaper when the raid began. The family thought he must have been burned to death in the building. After the raiders left town, the pitiful old father was seen raking the ashes in search of the bones of his boy, but no sign of the young man was ever found. Though John Speer, Jr., had been spared, one of his brothers had been shot before the Bullene home, so old John Speer, Sr., sustained a double loss that day.

Another strange escape was that of a man named Winchell. He ran into the home of Dr. Charles Reynolds, first minister of the Lawrence Episcopal Church, when chased by the raiders. The doctor was away, but there were three women in the house. Winchell was not killed by the implacable raiders, thanks to some quick thinking on the part of these three women. One of them quickly shaved off his whiskers, another found a lady's bonnet to put on his head, and they hustled him into a wheel chair beside a table covered with medicine bottles, spoons, and so forth. In reply to the questions of the outlaws the women said this was an ill aunt of Dr. Reynolds, come to Lawrence for treatment. The raiders stomped through the house, unable to find Mr. Winchell. Now and then one of them eyed the quilt-covered old woman in the wheel chair, but they made no attempt to investigate further. Sighs of relief came from the four persons in the house when the cursing raiders went away to continue their bloody mission at other houses.

A Mr. Bullene, whose residence was on New Hampshire Street, was away from his home at the time of the sacking, and only his wife and children were present. Being situated in the center of Lawrence, this house was used as a meeting place for the marauders. Captain George Todd ate breakfast there, and he promised Mrs. Bullene that her home would be spared from the flames. And so it was, although several times that day groups of the ruffians tried to set it afire and stopped when Mrs. Bullene told them that Captain Todd did not want it destroyed. One of the Bullene children, William, watched in horror while his young friend, the Speer lad, was shot. The boy fell to the ground but was still breathing when another outlaw rode up, reined in his plunging horse, and fired two more shots into the wounded boy's head—being sure then that he lay still and lifeless. The murderer espied Willie Bullene and took aim, but Mrs. Bullene rushed up and grabbed the horse's bridle while she explained again that Captain Todd had promised to protect them.

The mounted raiders shot at a young man in the next block, and he fell headlong into the gutter. His wife screamed and wept so violently that his would-be killers thought he was dead and galloped on. The young wife was relieved when her husband whispered, "Don't cry, darling. I don't think any of their bullets hit me." And so it proved. He had not been scratched.

Another such instance occurred when the Sargent home was burned. The young printer living there was fired at as he ran from the doomed house. When he fell close to the flaming building and lay there, the raiders supposed he was dead and raced on. After they were gone, rescuers found that he had not been hit. But he had been burned severely. Lying motionless close to the flames had taken severe discipline, but it had saved his life.

There were not many wounded who lived to tell about it. The outlaw riders nearly always returned to those they had shot and kept firing to make sure they were dead. Sometimes they fired into a pile of lifeless bodies, lest one or more of them still had a spark of life left. And their mistreatment of the wounded was incredibly heartless. They were so filled with hate and with a lust for killing that they seemed to enjoy killing a man by slow degrees. First a bullet in the shoulder, or arm, then another here and still another there, until the luckless victim was finally a corpse.

The thing that almost drove Quantrill mad was that the main object of his raid on Lawrence had escaped. General Lane had miraculously got away just in the nick of time. He well knew what would happen to him if he should fall into Quantrill's hands. At the first sign of the attack, Lane had fled from his house and dashed into a cornfield behind his home, had made his way through the large field and ridden to safety on a fleet-footed horse. To Mrs. Lane, Quantrill remarked, "Give your husband my compliments, madam, and tell him I should be most happy to meet him."

"That I will do sir," she replied. "I am sorry that it was not convenient for him to meet you this morning."

Gritting his teeth in rage, Quantrill and his men stomped out of the Lane parlor, set fire to the house, and then rode back to the center of Lawrence. Todd, Gregg, Colonel Holt, Bloody Bill Anderson, and others of his top men were assembled there, and they advised him that it was time to leave. They pointed

THE SACKING OF LAWRENCE

out that Federal cavalry was on the move from Kansas City, since someone had at last got word of the raid to the commandant there.

Quantrill agreed. "All right, men! Four hours of this is all any man can stand," he said. "Formation! Mount! We all ride for Missouri in a body!" he ordered.

He knew it would be safer for them to stick together, at least for this one time.

Quantrill was about right in his estimation of the time consumed in ravaging Lawrence. From all the accounts by survivors the attack began that morning at about five o'clock and the raiders left at approximately nine. It had been four hours of ruthless brutality, pillage, and murder. The business district had been burned first, all male citizens in sight had been killed; then the invaders had left the center of town and headed south, systematically killing and burning. When they finally left a smoking and ruined Lawrence, wild-eyed men and boys began to come out of hiding—but it was not all over yet.

Up to this time, not one of Quantrill's men had been killed. While they were riding on, headed back to Missouri, Larkin Skaggs, a former "hard shell" preacher who had turned bandit and who was now disgruntled because he felt he had not got his rightful share of the booty, wheeled his horse around and rode back to the City House.

The occupants of that spared building, thinking they were safe, were all standing out in front of the hotel, gazing in dismay at the ruin around them, when the lone rider came galloping back. He dashed up before the hotel, firing his revolver. He turned and started to ride away when a son of John Speer, whose little brother and an older brother had been murdered, picked up a rifle and fired at Skaggs. The shot hit its mark and brought Skaggs to the ground dead. (He never would have made it back to Missouri alive, anyhow, if on the return trip Quantrill had learned that his last volley killed Mr. Stone, Quantrill's friend at the City House.) Skaggs' body was dragged through the littered streets, then thrown into a ravine. No one offered to touch it or bury it.

Not all the guerrillas reached Missouri safely. Four wounded were captured near Lone Jack and hanged.

Back in Lawrence it was almost impossible to get exact figures concerning the dead or the amount of property damaged. A close accounting showed one hundred fifty-four of the best buildings in the business section and residential districts destroyed, with a property loss of a million and a half dollars, an appalling sum for those days. A hundred eighty-five men had died. The story of the sufferings and the heroism of those people of Lawrence will be told for generations to come.

Quantrill and his guerrillas struck out directly south, crossing the Wakarusa River at Blanton's Bridge, then went on through Prairie City, on their way to a retreat in the Sni Hills of Missouri. They made their escape to the headwaters of Little Blue River.

It seems incredible that three hundred armed killers were able to pass over forty miles of Kansas Territory by night and pounce at daybreak upon a town like Lawrence without any warning having been given. It seems still more incredible that these same men were able to accomplish their horrible purpose uninterrupted by any authorities, especially when Federal troops were close at hand. But such was the case. As a consequence, many gave Quantrill credit for being a master military mind.

After Lawrence

On leaving Lawrence, Quantrill learned that Colonel Preston B. Plumb, of Emporia, Kansas, commander of the 11th Kansas Volunteer Cavalry, was on the march from Kansas City, so he disbanded his men. He himself went into hiding in the home of a widow near Lexington, Missouri.

General Jim Lane gathered all available men and arms to follow Quantrill. When Colonel Plumb heard of Lane's citizen army, he countermarched and fell in between Quantrill's retreating guerrillas and Lane's men, expecting that the Federal troops at Paola would intercept the murderers, but nothing was accomplished except that the savageness of Quantrill's blow on Lawrence resounded around the world. The northern newspapers published a series of heated protests, and editorials urged that something drastic be done at once.

Governor Thomas Carney of Kansas wrote to Major General J. M. Schofield:

Leavenworth, Kans., August 24, 1863.
Sir: Disaster has again fallen on our State. Lawrence is in ashes. Millions of property have been destroyed, and, worse yet, nearly 200 lives of our best citizens have been sacrificed. No fiends in human shape could have acted with more savage barbarity than did Quantrill and his band in their last successful raid. I must hold Missouri responsible for this fearful, fiendish raid. No body of men large as that commanded by Quantrill could have been gathered together without the people residing in Western Missouri knowing everything about it. Such people cannot be considered loyal, and should not be treated as loyal citizens; for while they conceal the movements of desperadoes like Quantrill and his followers, they are, in the worst sense of the word, their aiders and abettors, and should be held equally guilty. There is no way of reaching these armed ruffians while the civilian is permitted to cloak him. . . .

As a result of this pressure, General Schofield wrote:

> Saint Louis, Mo., August 24, 1863
>
> Brigadier-General Ewing, Kansas City
>
> I will send six companies of the Eleventh Missouri Cavalry (240 men) to Sedalia, with orders to report to you. Send them orders at Sedalia. I will also direct General Brown to give you all the force he can spare temporarily. Would it not be well to call on the Governor of Kansas to furnish you a militia force to guard your posts a short time, so that your whole cavalry force can be put in the field after Quantrill? Spare no means by which he may be destroyed.

General Thomas Ewing then worried all night, trying to evolve a plan that would defeat Quantrill, and it seemed to him that the only way to catch the guerrillas was to starve them out. If he could arrange to remove all the support they were evidently receiving from the populace, they would soon run short not only of food but also of ammunition, and then they would make some desperate move which would betray them into his hands. In the fever of this night tension he conceived the idea of boldly denuding the countryside which had been sustaining the guerrillas, and therefore he issued his celebrated Order Number 11:

> Headquarters District of the Border,
> Kansas City, August 25, 1863.
>
> 1. All persons living in Jackson, Cass, and Bates Counties, and in that part of Vernon included in this district, except those living within one mile of the limits of Independence, Hickman's Mills, Pleasant Hill and Harrisonville; and except those in that part of Kaw Township, Jackson County, north of Brush Creek and west of Big Blue, are hereby ordered to remove from their present places of residence within fifteen days from the date hereof.
>
> Those who within that time establish their loyalty to the satisfaction of the comanding officer of the military station near their present place of residence will receive from him a certificate stating the fact of their loyalty, and the names of the witnesses by whom it can be shown. All who receive such certificates will be permitted to remove to any military station in this district, or to any part of

AFTER LAWRENCE

the State of Kansas, except the counties of the eastern border of the state. All others shall remove out of the district. Officers commanding companies and detachments serving in the counties named, will see that this paragraph is promptly obeyed.

2. All grain and hay in the field or under shelter, in the district from which inhabitants are required to move, within reach of military stations after the 9th day of September next, will be taken to such stations and turned over to the proper officers there, and report of the amount so turned over made to district headquarters, specifying the names of all loyal owners and the amount of such product taken from them. All grain and hay found in such district after the 9th day of September next, not convenient to such stations, will be destroyed.

3. The provisions of General Order Number 10 from these headquarters, will be at once vigorously executed by officers commanding in the parts of this district and at the station not subject to the operations of Paragraph One of this order, and especially the towns of Independence, Westport, and Kansas City.

4. Paragraph 3, Gen. Order No. 10, is revoked as to all who have borne arms against the Government in the district since the 20th day of August, 1863.

> By Order of Brigadier General Ewing.
> H. Hannahs, Adjutant General.

It was indeed a harsh and terrible order, and many innocent people suffered as a result of it. It was not long before roads and highways were filled with fugitives, decrepit old men and women, children and young boys. Their meager household goods were carted and pulled by old oxen and mules—animals of no use to the occupying Federals. Here and there in the pitiful procession were several sheep or a cow. Many families had pooled their three or four cows, because so many milk cows and sheep had been confiscated by the invading soldiers. The things the refugees were compelled to leave behind because they had no way of transporting their heavier belongings were sorted over by troops enforcing the removal notice, before the torch was set to everything.

Apologists for General Ewing claimed that the order came

directly from Major General Schofield at St. Louis and to him directly from Washington, D. C. In connection with this controversy here are excerpts from a personal letter to Ewing from Schofield as late as January 25, 1877:

A few unthinking people have, no doubt, supposed that the order was an act of retaliation for the massacre at Lawrence. Nothing could be more absurd. The farmers of Western Missouri were not regarded in anywise responsible for Quantrill's acts. Whether they were willing or not make no difference. If they raised crops, his men lived upon them, as did our troops when they had occasion. A large proportion of these citizens who were in good circumstances had voluntarily ceased this unprofitable purveying and had gone elsewhere. It was simply an act of dispassionate wisdom and humanity to stop it altogether. To call your order an act of inhumanity or of retaliation upon the people of Missouri is like accusing the Russian Commander of similar crimes against the people of Moscow when he ordered the destruction of that city to prevent its occupation as winter quarters of the army of Napoleon. . . .

It is simply justice to you, who have been censured by some for your celebrated order, to have this statement of the facts in regard to it. . . .

This would prove that Ewing issued the order of his own authority.

Federal Brigadier General George C. Bingham, a noted artist as well as a soldier, painted a picture which touchingly portrayed the suffering caused by Order Number 11, and he openly condemned Ewing. His painting of the burning of the people's household furnishings and the plundering of their houses showed the sky filled with flame and smoke and the long line of helpless and homeless people, with uniformed Federal officers rummaging in the trunks and furniture of the pillaged homesteads; captains gaudy with stolen jewelry. This picture created a sensation wherever it was exhibited. Bingham took it to Ohio when Ewing was running for governor of that state, and there can be no doubt that Bingham's speeches and the painting did much to defeat Ewing.

AFTER LAWRENCE

On February 22, 1877, Bingham wrote to the Jefferson City (Missouri) newspaper, *The Republican*:

I was present in Kansas City when the order was being enforced, having been drawn thither by the hope that I would be able to have it recinded, or at least modified; and I can affirm from painful personal observation that the sufferings of the unfortunate victims were such as should have elicited sympathy even from hearts of stone. Barefooted and bareheaded women and children, stripped of every article of clothing except a scant covering for their bodies, exposed to the heat of an August sun and struggling through the dust on foot. All their means of transportation had been seized by their spoilers, except an occasional dilapidated cart or an old superannuated horse, which were necessarily appropriated to the use of the aged and infirm.

It is well known that men were shot down in the very act of obeying the order, and their wagons and effects seized by their murderers. Large trains of wagons, extending over the prairies for miles in length, and moving Kansasward, were freighted with every description of household furniture and wearing apparel belonging to the exiled inhabitants. Dense columns of smoke arising in every direction marked the conflagrations of dwellings, many of the ruins can yet be seen, the chimneys standing scarred and blackened, the monuments of a ruthless military despotism which spared neither age, sex, character nor condition. No aid or protection was afforded to the banished inhabitants by the heartless authority which expelled them from their homes and their rightful possessions. They crowded by hundreds upon the banks of the Missouri River and were indebted to the charity of the benevolent steamboat conductors for transportation to places of safety where friendly aid could be extended to them without danger to those who ventured to contribute it. . . .

On the other hand, Quantrill himself did not receive such condemnation from his own side as General Ewing had to sustain for the rest of his life. As an indication of the attitude of the Southern authorities, a letter from Major General Nathaniel C. McLean is given here:

> Headquarters Price's Division
> Camp Bragg, Ark., November 2, 1863.

Col. William C. Quantrill,
 Commanding Cavalry:

Colonel: I am desired by Major-General Price to acknowledge the receipt of your report of your mark from the Missouri River to the Canadian, and that he takes pleasure in congratulating you and your gallant command upon the success attending it. General Price is very anxious that you prepare the report of your summer campaign. . . . He has been informed that orders of a most inhuman character were issued. Indeed, he has some emanating from those holding subordinate commands, but wants to have all the facts clearly portrayed, so that the Confederacy and the world may learn the murderous and uncivilized warfare which they themselves inaugurated, and thus be able to appreciate their cowardly shrieks and howls when a just retaliation the same "measure is meted out to them." He desires me to convey to you, and through you to your command, his high appreciation of the hardships you have so nobly endured and the gallant struggle you have made against despotism and the oppression of our State, with the confident hope that success will soon crown our efforts.

After the Lawrence massacre Quantrill acquired for himself a mistress, Kate King, who took on his middle name and thereafter was known as Kate Clarke. It was said that he virtually kidnapped her, carried her off to the hills and brush of Texas, but she seemed to like the treatment, for she continued to be involved with him until his death. Actually his star was waning, for the prodigious figures of George Todd and Bloody Bill Anderson were looming big on the horizon. It is from their ranks that the Jameses and the Youngers later arose to fame.

Left without Quantrill's leadership, some of his followers engaged in almost mortal combat among themselves. There had long been bad blood between Fletcher Taylor of Anderson's group and Captain William H. Gregg,* Quantrill's former aide-de-camp.

---

*It was this same Gregg who, after the war, penned a book on the life of Quantrill and sold it for several hundred dollars, which was

AFTER LAWRENCE

At the guerrilla camp in Mineral Springs, Texas, dissension arose and the disintegration of the command began. The growing popularity and power of George Todd as a leader greatly contributed to the unrest, although there were other things which further fired it. First and foremost, Todd's heart was in the cause for which he was fighting, and his influence over the men increased daily. Quantrill had fought for no ideal or principle, only for selfish purposes as a result of the conditions of his desperate life. When the supreme test for leadership arose, Todd in his devotion to the South and to his men won. Apparently Quantrill had long before seen his equal if not master in George Todd. After Todd's election by the men, Quantrill came to him and was very conciliatory, actually humble—unlike the tiger he had been.

Quantrill and his company were camped at Mineral Springs, near Sherman, Texas, when the restlessness became apparent. Perhaps it was the aftermath of Lawrence, or it could have been the ill feeling that arose among the members after the raids on Missouri City and Plattsburg. Gregg had told his men that if any money was taken it would be equally divided among them. But at Plattsburg Fletch Taylor and Little took about six thousand dollars in United States Government currency. The men were hard pressed at the time, and Gregg made no mention of the loot until they were safely across the Missouri River. He then asked about the money, and Taylor and Little refused to divide it. Gregg had a meeting with Quantrill and Todd at the home of Mrs. David George, and they made a demand on Taylor and Little for an equal division of the money. But Todd declared that Taylor and Little had a right to keep what they had taken, and Quantrill sided with Todd.

After that Bill Anderson married in Sherman, Texas, against the wishes of Quantrill, who wanted him to wait until peace

---

big money in those days. For some years it was supposed to be the only "true history" of the famous guerrilla chief; in later years it was proved to be a product of Gregg's vivid imagination. He had prepared a dozen so-called original manuscripts and sold them for substantial sums.

was declared. Anderson took leave of the camp, and his men followed him; they took up quarters in Sherman, leaving Quantrill at Mineral Springs. It was expected that Quantrill and Anderson would have to fight it out, and guards were posted around Sherman because the people wanted to prevent a surprise raid.

There were many killings and robbings, one that liquidated Andy Walker said to have been perpetrated by Fletch Taylor, Jim Chiles, and John Rose. Quantrill suggested that the men responsible should be court-martialed but Todd and Anderson refused to surrender the guilty men to the army authorities. When Major Butts, who lived just north of the town, was killed and robbed, Fletch Taylor, in admitting this was his work, protested that he had only been carrying out Quantrill's orders.

By now the demoralization of the guerrillas was complete. In Sherman they terrorized the people by riding pell-mell up and down the streets, firing their revolvers at random. On November 6, 1863, Colonel C. Franklin of the Provisional Army of the Confederate States of America, wrote to President Jefferson Davis to call attention "to some most unpleasant truths:

When Jo. Shelby, or any of the old jayhawking captains, makes a raid into Misouri, he and all his followers adopt the pirates' law of property. Mankind are considered but objects of prey, and, astonishing and painful as the knowledge must be, they rob indiscriminately friend and foe. If such work is not soon arrested, it may be continued indefinitely, for not a friend will be left in all that country to be ruined. Shelby boasts that on the last raid he completely "gutted Boonville"; also that many Southern families, hearing of his approach, had removed their goods out of doors, expecting him to burn their houses. In fact, sir, the Shelby-Marmaduke raids in that country have transferred to the Confederate uniform all the dread and terror which used to attach to the Lincoln blue. The last horse is taken from the widow and orphan, whose husband and father has fallen in the country's service. . . . On the other hand, General Steele, the Federal commander, is winning golden opinions for his forbearance, justice, and urbanity.

AFTER LAWRENCE

On Christmas Day of 1863 the guerrillas rode into the Christian Hotel and shot the ornaments off the cap of Mrs. Butts. They let their horses do much damage as they rode them into stores and other public buildings, destroying merchandise and other property. The Citizens' Committee complained to General Henry McCulloch (brother of Brigadier General Benjamin McCulloch who was killed at the Battle of Pea Ridge, Arkansas), and Bill Anderson, on hearing the many rumors, rode boldly into the camp of General McCulloch to inform him that Quantrill's men were responsible for the outrages.

On March 30, 1864, General McCulloch summoned Quantrill to his office and placed him under military arrest. He was told that his parole would be accepted and that he would not be confined in jail while awaiting trial. Quantrill was left with two guards in his room, his revolvers having been put on the bed, while the General went to dinner. On a pretext of getting a drink of water, Quantrill crossed the room, grabbed up the revolvers from the bed, and ordered his guards to surrender. He locked them in the clothes closet and left the room. But his attempt to escape was quickly discovered. He ran into three more guards on his way from the building, and it looked as if the game was up. But so desperate was the guerrilla leader that he seemed to possess the strength of a dozen men as he disarmed the guards and ran into the street, yelling at the top of his voice for his men to mount or they would all be arrested and shot.

Once more Quantrill seemed like the fearless leader of previous times. He sent a rider ahead to warn Todd of their danger and to tell him to break camp at once and meet him and the others at Colbert's Ferry.

Colonel J. Martin of the regular Confederate forces was ordered to pursue Quantrill and bring him back to Bonham dead or alive. "Bloody Bill" Anderson and his portion of the guerrillas joined in the mad ride after his former comrade. Todd and his men were waiting at the Bois d'Arc Creek, and they formed in the timber to check Martin's forces, while Quantrill and his followers rode by. Not long afterward, the forces of Todd and Quantrill crossed the Red River and escaped their pursuers. Not a single shot had been fired at the regular Confederate troops, for Todd had not permitted this. They had to trust to the speed of their horses to effect their escape.

Quantrill had accepted Todd's leadership, but of course under the surface he was bitterly resentful; and there were times when it appeared that even though Todd was in command Quantrill was still the real leader.

In the summer of 1864 Quantrill returned to Missouri and visited his old haunts. He could be seen roaming aimlessly over the desolated area where the inhabitants had been ruined by Ewing's Order Number 11. Quantrill rode on several minor skirmishes, but he never took part in any major fighting after his trip to Texas. His changed mood was just another unpredictable phase of the man's strange character.

Bloody Bill Anderson

Anderson and his band of sixty-five guerrilla fighters were resting for a short time in their hideaway in Northwestern Missouri in a heavily wooded section. The men sensed that something big was under way when "Captain" Anderson informed them that they would be riding to join General Sterling Price and his Confederate force within the next few days. Anderson was also making plans to feather his own nest, but no one saw any harm in this—least of all the Confederates.

In separating from Quantrill, Anderson had taken with him some sixty-five hand-picked ruffians, his friends, to form his own company of off-the-cuff fighters. Together, they carried on the guerrilla warfare in Missouri as they chose.

Many of those who knew him considered Anderson a demon—sadistic, cruel, brutal almost beyond belief. It was well known that he carried on his person a silken cord in which he tied a knot for each Union soldier he killed. At the time of his death there were more than fifty knots in the cord, so it was said. Certainly he was responsible for more deaths than that. He was fearless, ruthless, grim, taciturn, a man who asked no quarter and gave none. A silent man usually, when he did speak his voice cracked with authority. He had nothing but contempt for law and order.

In the town of Centralia, during one of the most horrifying incidents of the Civil War, "Captain" Anderson added a score or more knots to his silk cord.

On a sunny morning in September, 1864, at the camp of Captain Tom Todd, only a few miles from the hiding place of Anderson and his men, breakfast was not quite over when an excited sentry dashed in, calling out, "Captain Todd! Captain

Todd! A big company of horsemen is coming in this direction, sir! I don't know if they're Federals or not."

Captain Tom Todd was on his feet instantly and giving orders to his men. He formed them near the road and galloped his horse, alone, to see for himself whether the aproaching riders were friends or foes. In a short time he was seen returning at leisure, talking with a man who undoubtedly was the leader of the company which had so aroused the camp and caused the men to assume fighting positions. Captain Tom Todd rode directly to where his men were hidden and called them to come into view.

"Men," he said, "this is Captain George Todd. He has a company of eighty men and is looking for the camp of Bill Anderson. He's a Todd, but so far we haven't been able to determine any relationship between us."

The men of Captain Tom Todd's company looked George Todd over carefully. He had all the appearance of a fighter. He was of Scottish descent, medium build, and, though he was more cautious than the reckless Bloody Bill Anderson, he fought with a dogged determination that threw terror into the ranks of his enemy. His men never doubted his leadership. He was more talkative than Anderson was and when agitated could swear heartily.

The two Todds, the morning after their meeting, crossed with their men into Howard County and made camp in an area known as Elgin's pasture. Late that afternoon, a brother of Tom Todd, N. P. Todd, rushed into camp to inform his brother that about a hundred soldiers were on the road, marching toward Rocheport.

"Come on, men! On your horses!" yelled the two Todds to their forces. "We'll give 'm something to remember!"

In less time than it takes to tell it, one hundred and thirty armed guerrillas were speeding on their way to intercept the enemy. Eight abreast, they charged upon the stunned Federals. George Todd's men, as always, were in front. It was indeed true, as the Federals said about George: "That man is a tiger!

He fights always; he isn't happy unless he's fighting. He will have to be killed to be stopped."

From long practice the guerrillas had acquired a skill and cunning that seemed uncanny. They were so fast, so reckless of danger, and their use of the revolver was so expert and deadly that their onset was well-nigh irresistible. Their frightful charge with guns and an ear-splitting rebel yell caused their opponents to break ranks in confusion.

Those Union soldiers on horseback were hotly pursued by the shrieking men of George Todd, and they dashed madly for cover, reaching a wooded, brushy area too quickly for the guerrillas to inflict much loss of life. Like rabbits they scattered in every direction. The golden haze of Indian summer lay on the land, casting generous but futile beams of warmth upon the bodies of the dead Union soldiers. The slain that day numbered nearly thirty, and their corpses were left strewn along the country lane. The general order of attack had been, as always, "Aim low, keep cool, fire when you get loaded. Let the wounded lie until the fight is over." Now the crisp autumn grass crackled under foot as Arch Clements inspected the fallen bodies. Not another shot was needed—all the men were dead. Only one of the guerrillas had been wounded.

Since it was useless to chase the Federals into the brush, they took what would be useful to them from the Union supply train and set the torch to the wagons. Then they rode into camp some ten miles south of Fayette.

The following day Captain Bill Anderson and his men joined the forces of the two Todds. The main group of the guerrillas had learned that General Price was making his way toward Jefferson City, and they hoped to catch up with him and join forces with him before night.

But darkness closed in too soon, and the guerrillas made camp and that night held a council of war. Anderson, ever eager for a fight, declared, "By gad, we can still raid through Howard and Boone Counties, tear up railroad tracks, cut telegraph wires, and reach Price in time!"

"We'll just raise hell in general," agreed George Todd. "We have to keep in practice, you know."

The men sitting around laughed uproariously. They were all in high fettle and fighting spirits. Their plan of operation, naturally, was to draw the main body of Federal soldiers away from the river, so that they—the guerrillas—might retrace their tracks and cross the river in comparative safety.

The next day the entire group headed for Rocheport. After an hour's ride Anderson said, "Fayette is just ahead, men. How about giving the town a little excitement?"

This suggestion was met with whoops and yells of joy from the band.

Anderson smiled dryly and said, "Not so long ago a bunch of them damn Yankees surprised six of my men in a barn and killed them all, so we can settle that score real quick."

George Todd advised against this sortie, but Bloody Bill was determined to have his way and ordered a charge when they got to Fayette. The two Todds rode around to the left, and Anderson and his men went to the right of the courthouse. The guerrillas were well in town before the Federals were aware of their presence. Then, yelling like a tribe of drunken Indians and shooting wildly in every direction, they charged through the surprised town. The Union soldiers sent a volley of gunfire at the raiders, and they retreated, but only for a few minutes. Converging northwest of the town, they reformed their ranks and made another furious charge.

By this time the soldiers had stationed themselves in an old log house, some nearby brick buildings, and a deep gulley. They poured such a deadly fire into the ranks of the guerrillas that they had to beat a hasty retreat.

"Damn their blue-bellied hides!" roared Anderson. "It's damned lucky for us that they can't shoot straight, or we'd be a bloody pulp by now!"

And he was right, for the Federals were armed with short-barreled, long-range rifles. Anderson still refused to give up, and he ordered the men to make charge after charge under a heavy fire at point-blank range. He did not quit until six of the guerrillas had been killed. He cursed and raved that there were now another six that the damn Yankees would have to pay dearly for.

The two Todds shook their heads in silence. It was easy to see, now, that there would have to be an election of one officer to command all three companies—and heaven help them if Anderson were chosen! A council was held, and the leader chosen was George Todd, one of the few guerrillas who really fought for a principle and not for personal gain.

Early the following morning they were on the march toward Huntsville. When they got near the town, two of the guerrillas were sent in to demand the immediate surrender of the town. The ruffians were advised to come in and take it if they wanted it badly. When it came to a threatened attack by guerrillas, the townsfolk throughout Missouri banded together against their common enemy. Personal quarrels and difficulties were forgotten at such a time of danger. However, people of Southern sympathies were not expected to fire upon regular Confederate troops.

Captain George Todd took one good look at the town of Huntsville and said, "Come on, men, let's travel away from this place. As you can see, these houses are like those in Fayette, and I am trying to forget that incident. Let's travel on."

Anderson's resentment at being overruled showed in the grim set of his jaw and the smoldering light in his eyes; but his hard mouth was closed tight as he rode on past the town of Huntsville. The following morning the guerrillas were a few miles southeast of Centralia, Missouri, in a wooded overnight camping place. The men joked and laughed, stretched out lazily on the grass, using their saddles for pillows while they talked of past adventures and coming days. Little did any of those hardened men suspect that Union troops were in the vicinity, as they boasted that they could outfight and outrun any damn Federals.

The Unionists had once declared, "Quantrill sometimes spares. Anderson never!" Anderson's men thought of this that morning when their chief came walking toward them, tall, gaunt, saturnine. He had grown restless as well as resentful toward the Todds. His voice cracked with authority as he spoke.

"Saddle your horses, men. We'll do some riding this morning, and see how the land lays over in Centralia."

The Battle of Centralia

It was close to ten o'clock that cloudy morning of September 27, 1864, when in a haze of dust and the sound of galloping horses' hoofs a company of men rode boisterously into the Missouri town of Centralia. Some of them wore long linen dusters; others were in uniforms of various types; so at first the citizens were not sure just who they were or why they were entering their peaceful little town. They did notice, however, that the rough-appearing riders were heavily armed with a sinister array of big Navy Colts in their belts or waistbands. Most of the motley company wore their unkempt hair long, almost to their shoulders.

Then it was whispered around by some of the citizens on the main street that the hard-visaged man commanding the company was none other than the notorious Bloody Bill Anderson.

"The guerrillas!" men and women exclaimed, and they fled into their houses.

When the invaders entered the stores and began looting them, most of the storekeepers and other businessmen fled out the back way, thinking not of their goods so much as of their lives.

Anderson walked erectly and brazenly into a saloon, where he and his men took over the place. They broke open a barrel of whiskey and began drinking it, using shoes and women's slippers in lieu of glasses or cups, the new shoes having been taken from one of the nearby stores.

In high glee Anderson shouted, "Drink up, fellows! But don't get drunk. Them's my orders, and you'd better obey 'em!"

When the drinking orgy was at its height, the Columbia stagecoach arrived in Centralia, bound for Mexico, Missouri, where the passengers were to attend a political meeting. Inside the stage were some prominent persons: Major James Rollins (a member of Congress), James H. Waugh (sheriff of Boone County, afterwards a well-known banker), John M. Samuel (a former sheriff), Henry Keane, Boyle Gordon, Lewis Shaw, and Lafayette Hume. The stage was brought to a halt by the outlaws and all the passengers were robbed of their money, jewelry, or other valuables. Anderson's greed made no distinction between Northerners and Southerners when he robbed. But the occupants of the stagecoach had saved their lives by giving false names to the raiders.

The stagecoach was then permitted to proceed on its way. A short time before noon the regular westbound passenger train of the Wabash Railroad was expected. The guerrillas dragged up crossties and threw them upon the rails, and concealed themselves. The engineer, seeing the obstructions, and also noting that sections of the town were afire, brought his train to a stop. The raiders fell in on each side of the train, firing their heavy revolvers and threatening the engineer and other trainmen with instant death. Anderson and his men went through all the coaches and took off twenty-two Federal soldiers, some of them ill and others being mustered out of service.

Lieutenant Peters saw what was happening; he quickly took off his uniform and cap, wrapped a blanket about himself and darted out under the burning depot. He was captured by two of the guerrillas and led to the spot where the execution of the soldiers was to take place. Of the twenty-four soldiers of the Union Army who had been on the train, only one escaped death. He was Sergeant Goodman, who was kept alive as a hostage, to be offered in exchange for Cave Wyatt, one of Anderson's men who had been captured a short time before while on a train en route to St. Louis.

The other poor wretches were marched to the edge of town and lined up, and it is said that Anderson himself shot all of them, a fresh-loaded pistol being handed to him as fast as he emptied the one in hand. No amount of pleading saved a single life, and not one word of pity or protest was uttered by

THE BATTLE OF CENTRALIA

any of the guerrillas. On the contrary, they all seemed to gloat over the ruthless massacre of the Union soldiers by their monster chieftain.

After taking from the train everything of value they could carry off, Anderson's men set it afire, ordered the engineer to start the engine, pull the throttle wide open, and jump off. The engineer uncoupled the engine after the cars had burned, and farther up the road gathered the terrified and injured passengers into the cab and tender of the locomotive and rushed them to the town of Sturgeon. The soldiers in that town, on hearing the story, hurriedly prepared for an attack. But they tried to strengthen their position instead of going out at once and fighting off the guerrillas. They had heard that Major A. E. V. Johnson and three hundred soldiers were en route to Centralia, and they thought it better judgment to let the regular army take care of the murderers.

Great apprehension prevailed in the little town of Sturgeon, where it was feared Anderson's men would attack next. But late that afternoon a lone rider came galloping into town. He was unarmed, and his uniform was in tatters, literally torn from his body. Only the remaining shreds and pieces of his pants identified him as having been one of Johnson's command. The soldier was on the verge of collapse from shock and exhaustion. He told haltingly of the fighting in Centralia, the killing of citizens, the looting of the stores and homes, and the burning of the town. Many of the troops had been pursued almost to Sturgeon and killed. The people went out and got the bodies and brought them to Sturgeon and placed them in the church, which was converted into a morgue suddenly.

Some apologists for Bloody Bill Anderson have claimed that his slaughter of the soldiers at Centralia was in retaliation for the Palmyra affair as previously narrated in this book. Nevertheless, it was not in Anderson's makeup to spare a Union soldier, regardless of the circumstances. We should remember, too, that even before the outbreak of the Civil War Anderson had been the leader of a band of horsethieves and robbers.

The cold-blooded murder of the soldiers taken from the

train in Centralia has gone down in history as one of the most atrocious crimes of the era.

Major Johnson, who was stationed at Paris, in Monroe County, received news of Anderson's attack on Centralia when it first began. He believed that Todd's men also were with Bloody Bill, and he made plans to attack them all. He came upon their trail south of Middle Grove and followed it into the town where he found the bodies of the dead soldiers and the town in ruins. Furiously Johnson ordered an attack on the guerrillas who were then only a few miles away. He had received definite orders from General Clinton B. Fisk to weed out all the guerrillas in his territory.

Had the Major known of the deadly accuracy of the guerrillas, their swift, terrible maner of charging a foe, and their death-dealing revolvers, he might have wisely chosen to ride to Sturgeon and safety, might have allowed the raiders to remain unmolested. But he had not seen or met that kind of enemy in combat. The guerrillas' habit was to go into battle at full gallop, and when in gun range of the enemy to let loose with a terrifying rebel yell, which alone was enough to curdle the blood. And with increasing speed they let go with a deadly barrage of heavy caliber bullets, often firing with both hands. They always carried several loaded cylinders tied to their saddle horns or in their pockets, and when a revolver was empty they had some kind of trick (practiced and perfected) whereby the empty gun cylinder was knocked out and the loaded one swiftly injected. Their aim was perfect, and most of their victims died shot through the head.

Major Johnson, sitting his fine horse, rode down Centralia's main business street, his impressive regiment close behind. Suddenly a young woman dashed out into the street, threw her arms about the neck of his horse, begging him not to fight Anderson's guerrillas.

"Those devils will kill all of you, sir! I beg of you, turn around and run for your lives! I saw what Anderson and his gang did here today, and it was ghastly beyond description. Please retreat before it is too late, Major!"

Johnson was impressed by her pleas, but he replied calmly, "My good woman, much as I appreciate your concern, I have orders to attack those cutthroat guerrillas. Surely you would not have our soldiers run from those murderous swine. Look what they did to your beautiful town. They must be annihilated, so that their outrages cannot continue. Do not worry, Miss. We will bring Anderson's head back on a rail within a few hours."

With that Major Johnson and his forces rode out of Centralia on the trail of the guerrillas.

At that same time Captain George Todd had sent a scout to ascertain the strength of Johnson's troops and his armament. The scout, John Thrailkill, through his field glasses saw one hundred three in line, two abreast, making a total of two hundred six men, armed with what appeared to be Enfield muskets. This information was conveyed to Captain Todd, who sent an order to Thrailkill to decoy the enemy to their position. Todd ordered his main detachment to fall back into the timber and gave instructions for them to charge at his signal. Todd then went up on a rise where he could get a clear view of the Federals and at the same time be seen by his own men. Captain Tom Todd waited, ready on the left with fifty men, and Anderson with his sixty-five picked men stayed to the right, with Captain George Todd's company of eighty men forming the center. It was always George Todd's decision to take the center of an attack, and this time was no exception.

Thrailkill and his ten men rode up close to Centralia and exchanged a few shots with the Federals. Johnson sent out a number of men to attack them, when the wily Thrailkill fell back for a mile, then wheeled and charged the soldiers, sending them scampering. At that Johnson left about twenty men to guard the wagons, mounted the balance of his soldiers, and started in hot pursuit, with Thrailkill pausing now and then to exchange a few shots while he led the Federals on into the Todd ambush. It is difficult to understand why Johnson could have been maneuvered into such a trap, as he must have known that Todd's main body of troops was nearby and he should have suspected that the purpose of this small group of guerrillas was to lead him somewhere.

When about three miles from town, Major Johnson ordered three-fifths of his men to dismount, leaving every fourth man to hold four horses, as was the custom with mounted infantry. At the same time Thrailkill had ridden up to Captain Todd, who was standing on the rise watching. Now Thrailkill and the ten men with him dismounted and tightened their saddle girths for the main charge. This act possibly gave Johnson the idea that Todd and Anderson planned to fight on foot. He should have known better than that. The guerrillas, with years of mounted warfare to their names, certainly would not now resort to infantry tactics.

Major Johnson, riding in front of his foot soldiers, came forward about a half mile. He raised his saber and shouted, "Why don't you come back and fight instead of running like scared rabbits, you women-killing bastards!"

Calmly Todd waited to allow Johnson ample distance away from his horses before he ordered an attack. Then—Todd raised his hat and replaced it on his head three times, the prearranged signal. One can imagine the surprise and consternation of the Union troops when they saw the three companies come galloping over the rise, many of the riders with their horses' reins in their teeth, a heavy Dragoon revolver in each hand! When they were within range of the guns of the enemy, the familiar and blood-chilling rebel yell was raised. The soldiers fired a volley at eighty yards, most of the bullets going harmlessly over the heads of the advancing guerrillas, killing only three of them and wounding three.

When they were forty yards in front of the huddled Union soldiers, the entire front of the on-racing horde looked like a solid mass of flame from their guns. The smoke rose and disclosed fifty-seven dead soldiers on the ground, the rest in wild flight. In short order they, too, were prone on the ground, motionless in death. Major Johnson also was dead, having been singled out by the young fellow who later became famous as a bandit, Jesse James. For just one shocked moment the

THE BATTLE OF CENTRALIA

soldiers who had been left holding the horses stood as though petrified, as though they had seen a ghostly legion appear out of nowhere. Then they turned and galloped madly away, with the guerrillas in hot pursuit. Anderson led the charge against those who were left, and those soldiers also were shot down.

One of Johnson's men who miraculously escaped the carnage told the vivid story in Sturgeon. He said that the road all the way from Centralia to Sturgeon was strewn with dead soldiers. Later, when the people of both towns went out to see for themselves, they found so many corpses on the dusty road that they might have thought a terrible plague had swept over the land. Of Major Johnson's force only fifteen or eighteen escaped.

This battle had repercussions: Generals Douglass and Fisk countermanded the order to kill all guerrillas and take no prisoners; henceforth they would be treated as prisoners of war.

That afternoon the guerrilla bands crossed the river at Rocheport and joined the army of General Sterling Price as they had set out to do.

Deaths of Todd and Anderson

In 1864 twenty-five-year-old Captain Herman Wagner, a German who was commander of the Second Colorado Cavalry, U.S.A., in Independence boasted that he would bring Quantrill in on a board in short order. Arrogant and self-assured, he declared, "Yah, in vun hurry we vill fix dot feller veneffer he comes here. Dot Qvantrill, he vill be a dead vun!"

Colonel Curtis, retreating before General Price toward Independence, held the western bank of the Little Blue, entrenched behind stone walls and fences. General Jo Shelby broke Curtis' hold on those improvised fortifications and pressed him back through the town of Independence, with Wagner and his cavalry protecting Curtis' rear troops and doing a good job at it.

Toward the end of that day, October 23rd, Captain Wagner led his company to the crest of the hill near Sugar Creek, and that is where the gallant George Todd fell, his neck pierced by a Spencer rifle ball. His companions tenderly carried him to the house of a Mrs. Burns, where he died a few hours later. Before his death—at only twenty-five—Todd embraced the Roman Catholic faith, as Quantrill later did before his death.

"We will bury him in the town cemetery," said young Jesse James. "Then nobody will bother him, and we will always know where George is."

The guerrillas all agreed, and the earthly remains of George Todd were buried in the most convenient lot, which happened to be the burial plot of the Beatty family. Beatty came hurrying to the cemetery when he learned what was going on.

"I want no such riffraff in my family lot!" he cried. "If you bury him here, he won't remain there long, I assure you."

Thrailkill and McCoy gave Beatty a menacing scowl, but the

youthful Jesse James spoke up: "If you dare to dig up George's body, old man, we'll come back here and put you in that empty grave."

Beatty recoiled as though he had met a rattlesnake in his path. To this day, George Todd lies buried where he was placed in 1864. Along the driveway which passes through the cemetery, but a very short distance from the impressive Beatty monument, is a marker with the following inscription:

> George W. Todd, 2nd Lieut.
> Quantrill's Co., Mo. Cav.
> C.S.A., October 23, 1864 . . .

and sticking in the ground near the marker is a small Confederate battle flag.

Such is the irony of fate, the boastful Captain Wagner and seventeen of his cavalry soldiers were buried that same day—in the same cemetery in Independence.

For many months the Federal authorities exerted every effort to capture Bloody Bill Anderson. One of Anderson's greatest prides was fine horses. He liked to get a beautiful unbroken horse or mare and train the animal himself. He was always riding about on some spirited horse, and when leading his band he invariably rode way out in front of his column on his dancing, prancing mount.

On October 27, 1864, Anderson was riding an especially magnificent newly acquired mare, leading his guerrilla column, when without warning he saw both sides of the trail lined with armed Union soldiers. Even before he had a chance to draw one of his big revolvers, his body was riddled with bullets from the terrific crossfire, and he plunged from his frightened mount, dead. In so dying, Anderson saved his entire command from destruction, for he was far out in front of them. By thus forcing the Federal troops to show their hand before the main body of guerrillas rode up, he unwittingly enabled them to scatter. Several heroic attempts were made by his followers to recover the body of their leader, but to no avail.

Anderson's death occurred just a half mile north of the little town of Orrick, Missouri, in the southwest corner of Ray County. The Union soldiers took the body in a wagon to Richmond, Missouri, where they displayed their intense hatred for the guerrilla chieftain by cutting off his head and dragging the decapitated body through the streets behind a horse. Some of the citizens of Richmond were sickened by this barbarism, and they requested that the remains be turned over to them for burial, but this request was ignored. Bill's head was placed on top of a spiked telegraph pole and left there for hours, as a warning to all other guerrillas. The Union soldiers celebrated the demise of their archenemy, and that night when most of them were drunk the burial request was granted.

The body and its head were buried in the graveyard in the northeast part of town. For a long time that grave was only that of a forgotten man, weed-grown, untended, seldom visited except by an occasional ex-guerrilla. But some years ago the Mormons took over this cemetery, and ever since it has been well maintained.

Not until 1908 was the long-delayed funeral service for Bloody Bill Anderson held. That year Cole Younger went to Richmond with his carnival and his "Hell on the Border" wax museum, and he heard from a Richmond attorney, J. L. Farris, Jr., that Anderson had been buried there without benefit of clergy. Cole's heart was touched, and he immediately took steps to remedy this neglect. His carnival musicians furnished the music, and the Reverend J. E. Dunn said a prayer at the grave. The lawyer, Farris, presented an appropriate little talk, as did Cole Younger who spoke of the bravery and unselfishness of Bill Anderson, and of how all his men had loved him.

As the *Richmond Missourian* of June 11, 1908, said:

. . . Mr. Farris spoke for some twenty minutes, paying tribute to the power of endurance, courage and daring of the dead soldier. He said that it was time to cover the dust of the hero with flowers of affection and honor.

Taps was sounded, and many a moist eye was in evidence, especially those of several old-timers who had known Anderson during his hectic career. The rites were concluded with the impressive draping of the Stars and Stripes with the Stars and Bars. There was such a hush that it seemed the warble of a river thrush far distant could be heard.

The Last of Quantrill

After the death of George Todd and Bill Anderson, the guerrillas fully realized that their cause was lost. General Price's great raid had been a failure, and therefore they were no longer afforded the protection of a Confederate armed force in Missouri. So they agreed to disband.

Rumor had it (on good authority) that Quantrill was obsessed with a scheme to go to Washington and murder President Lincoln. When he heard that John Wilkes Booth had done the job, he remarked, "Good! Now I am saved the trouble!"

This is only another example of Quantrill's venomous nature. He had held his followers because of his cleverness and his fast thinking in emergencies, but he was never really liked, not even by his closest associate, William H. Gregg, who had long been his aide-de-camp. Actually the famed guerrilla chief seemed to be a man out of place, a man who ought to have lived in some savage land centuries ago, for he held human life as cheaply as ever did Attila the Hun or Genghis Khan, the Mongolian leader of savage hordes that once ravaged Asia. Like those cruel despots, Quantrill thought no more of taking the life of a man than he did of snuffing out the life of an insect underfoot.

Yet he was possessed of an eloquent tongue, and he easily conveyed the idea to his followers that he was on earth for the purpose of exterminating the "damn Yankees." Of course, there is no slightest doubt of his daring and bravery, or of his ability as a guerrilla leader. He fought like a demon, a fixed grin on his face, his eyes blazing with the lust to kill. There is no evidence that he even believed in God; yet, strangely

THE LAST OF QUANTRILL

enough, when he lay on his deathbed he embraced the Roman Catholic faith and received the last rites of that church.

One of his many odd quirks was his false claim to membership in the Masonic order. William Gregg, himself a Mason, would have known if Quantrill had been a Mason. When questioned about this Gregg replied, "If so, he never made himself known as such." It is probable that Quantrill fictitiously represented himself as a member of the brotherhood only when he hoped it would secure him help in a difficult spot. There is no record that he at any time belonged to that organization.

At White River, Arkansas, Quantrill and forty-eight of his men parted company with Shepherd's men (including Jesse James) who were going to Texas. Quantrill and his own company turned toward Kentucky. They were wearing the blue Union uniforms as a disguise and they had no trouble in passing through the Union Army lines. They planned to get to Kentucky by way of Hart County, Marion County, New Market, bypassing Bradford, and on to Houstonville. There were quite a lot of Federal soldiers at that point, and they had many fine horses; Quantrill and his men felt they themselves could use fresh mounts. Quantrill went to the hotel to chat with the commandant of the post, while his men set about stealing the horses. An excited Union Army corporal rushed into the hotel to inform his superior that Union soldiers, and strangers at that, were riding off on the best horses in the corral.

Quickly the Major strapped on his revolvers and went dashing out of the hotel, followed by the smiling Quantrill. One of the guerrillas was riding up on a splendid horse, and the Major demanded that he dismount at once. Only one ending could come from such a situation in which a Quantrill rider was involved—the Major was shot dead even as he fumbled for one of his guns to enforce his command. Quantrill, his men and himself mounted on the finest horses, went gaily galloping on his way.

At Hartford, Kentucky, Quantrill, still dressed as a Federal officer, induced the commandant of the Kentucky Militia, Captain Frank Barnette, to go with him to trail the Kentucky guerrillas, the notorious Marion and Sue Mundy. Taking with him thirty of his soldiers, Barnette accompanied Quantrill, all unaware that his new acquaintance was seeking a chance to destroy his whole company. While they were crossing a shallow stream, Frank James rode up to Captain Barnette and shot him in the head, killing him instantly. This was the planned signal for a quick extermination of the detachment of soldiers.

Early in May Quantrill started for Salt River with William Hulse, John Ross, Clark Hockinsmith, Isaac Hall, Richard Glasscock, Robert Hall, Bud Pence, Allen Parmer, Dave Helton, Lee McMurtry, and Payne Jones. When they were near the post office of Smiley, Kentucky, a terrific rainstorm came up, and the guerrillas sought shelter in the barn of a man named Wakefield, a few miles out from the town of Smiley. Quite by accident, a cavalry detachment under the command of Captain Edward Terrell, who held an undying hatred for Quantrill and his outlaws, passed along the roadway and noticed the tracks in the mud which had been left by Quantril's band as they turned into the barn.

Glasscock was the first to see the column of Union Cavalrymen coming, but before the guerrillas could saddle up the soldiers were storming the barn. Quantrill shouted for every man to take care of himself and to meet him at a given point. Ross, Hulse, Parmer, Pence, and McMurtry were able to mount and cut their way through the Federal ranks, firing right and left as they went. Quantrill was in the barnyard, trying without success to mount his spirited horse. Hockinsmith rushed to his chief's aid, and both men attempted to escape on Hockinsmith's horse. A volley of gunfire from the cavalrymen killed Hockinsmith and the horse, spilling Quantrill to the ground. In the meantime, the Halls, Helton, and Jones were able to flee on foot into the adjacent timberland. Glasscock, who was mounted, rushed back in an effort to save Quantrill, but another volley killed him and mortally wounded Quantrill, who was struck by two Spencer balls, one in the hand, the other

THE LAST OF QUANTRILL

entering and shattering the collar bone and ranging downward along the spine, paralyzing him from the waist down.

The dying guerrilla chieftain was carried into the Wakefield house. He was conscious and able to gasp to the owner of the house that he was dying, and he asked to be allowed to remain there to die. In the meantime the escaping guerrillas met the remainder of their band at Sayers, about twenty miles from the Wakefield place, and relayed the grave news. It was the end of the trail for the Missouri guerrillas, who resumed their journey into Kentucky merely because they had nowhere else to go.

Quantrill had advised his men that, in the event of such disaster, they should surrender at once—and this they did, to Captain C. Young of the U. S. Army Regulars, at Samuel's Depot, Nelson County, Kentucky, on July 26, 1865.

General I. Palmer, in charge of the Department of Kentucky, feared that Quantrill's men would still try to seize their leader from the Wakefield house, so he had Quantrill transferred to a military hospital in Louisville. Until it was definitely established that he had no possible chance to recover, he was allowed no visitors. A Catholic priest finally persuaded the authorities to permit him to move Quantrill to the Catholic hospital in Louisville, and on June 6th, at four in the afternoon, the notorious guerrilla leader expired, a Catholic in good standing.

Some people claimed that Quantrill escaped and did not die of his wounds; but this is not in accordance with the records of the United States Army and the Roman Catholic Church. He was buried in St. John's Catholic Cemetery, formerly called the Portland Cemetery. In December of 1887, W. W. Scott removed his remains to his old home town, Canal Dover, Ohio, for reinterment in the Quantrill family cemetery lot. It is said that Scott retained a piece of Quantrill's arm bone for a relic.

Quantrill's will bequeathed all his earthly possessions to his mistress, Kate King known as Kate Clarke. She took the money to St. Louis where she established herself as the madam of one of the most famous bawdy houses of that era.

Roster of Guerrillas

After long and tedious research the writer is able to append to this history a verified and complete list of the names of the men who, at one time or another, rode with Quantrill.

A
Akers, Sylvester
Anderson, James (Killed in Austin, Texas, after the war)
Anderson, William (Killed at Orrick, Missouri, in 1864)
Archie, Hugh
Archie, William
Asbury, A. E.

B
Baker, John (Orderly sergeant)
Barker, John
Barnhill, John
Basham, Sol
Basham, William (Surrendered at Smiley, Kentucky)
Berry, Dick
Berry, Ike
Bishop, John
Bledsoe, William (Killed on retreat at Lawrence)
Blunt, Andy (Wounded, April 16, 1862)
Blythe, Christian name unknown
Bochman, Charley
Brady, Matt (Captured)
Brady, Christian name unknown
Brinker, Jim
Broomfield, Ben
Bunch, Oliver
Burns, Dick (Hanged, May 27, 1867)
Burton, Pete (Killed at Lamar, Missouri, November 5, 1862)

C
Campbell, Doc

ROSTER OF GUERRILLAS

Carr, Bill (Killed April 16, 1862)
Carter, Harrison
Castle, Theodore
Chatman, John
Chiles, Bill
Chiles, James Crow (Killed by a citizen at Independence)
Chiles, Kit
Clarke, Jerome H. (Sue Mundy) (Hanged at Louisville, Kentucky)
Clarke, Sam C.
Clayton, George
Clifton, Sam
Clements, Arch (Killed at Lexington, Missouri, December, 1866)
Clements, Henry
Commons, Smith
Corum, Al
Corum, James
Corum, John
Crabtree, Joe
Crawford, Riley (Killed in Jackson County, Missouri)
Creth, Creek
Cummins, Jim (Died in Confederate Home, Higginsville, Missouri, around 1928)
Cundhill, Christian name unknown
Cunningham, Abe

D

Dalton, J. Frank (Died, Granbury, Texas, 1951)
Dalton, Kit
Dancer, Jim
De Bonhorst, Paul
De Hart, E. P.
Devers, Alva
Devers, Art
Donohue, Jim (Killed, Lamar, Missouri, 1862)

E

Edmundson, J. F.
Emory, Jeff
Ervin, J. C.
Esters, Josh

Estes, Christian name unknown
Evans, Tom (Surrendered at Smiley, Kentucky)

F

Farretts, John
Flannery, Ike (Killed by Jesse James after the war)
Flannery, John
Flannery, Si
Flournoy, John
Fox, Christitan name unknown
Freeman, Will
Frisby, John
Fry, Frank

G

Gaw, Bill (Went to Kentucky with Quantrill)
George, Dave
George, Gabe (Killed at Independence, Missouri, February 1862)
George, Hicks
George, Hiram (Captain in Quantrill's band)
Gibson, Joe
Gilchrist, Joe (Killed at Pink Hill, Missouri, April 1862)
Glasscock, Richard (Killed May 10, 1865, in Kentucky)
Gordon, Silas
Graham, John (Went to Kentucky with Quantrill)
Gray, Frank
Greenwood, William (Became prosperous Missouri farmer)
Gregg, Frank J. (Settled in Independence, Missouri, after the war)
Gregg, William H. (Adjutant, Quantrill's Guerrillas)
Guess, Hiram

H

Haick, Christian name unknown
Hall, Isaac (Went to Kentucky with Quantrill)
Hall, Robert (Went to Kentucky with Quantrill)
Hall, Thomas (Went to Kentucky with Quantrill)
Haller, Abe
Haller, Wash
Haller, William (Quantrill's first recruit)
Hamilton, Sam
Hamlett, Jesse

ROSTER OF GUERRILLAS

Hampton, John
Harris, John
Harris, Reuben (Harbored Quantrill's men)
Harris, Tom
Harrison, Christian name unknown
Hart, Joseph
Hays, Perry
Hays, William
Hegan, Edward
Helms, Polk
Hendricks, James A.
Henry, Thomas
Higbee, Charles
Hildebrand, Sam (Killed March 21, 1872, at Pinckneyville, Illinois)
Hill, Thomas
Hill, Tucker
Hill, Woot
Hines, John
Hink, Edward
Hinton, Christian name unknown
Hockinsmith, Clarke (Killed May 10, 1865, in Kentucky)
Hillings, Washington
Holt, John
Hoy, Perry (Executed at Fort Leavenworth, Kansas)
Hubbard, John
Hudspeth, George (Babe) (Went part way to Kentucky with Quantrill)
Hudspeth, Rufe (Went part way to Kentucky with Quantrill)
Huffaker, Mose
Hulse, William (Went to Kentucky with Quantrill)
Hunt, Thomas (Guerrilla Tom) (Was mistaken for Jesse James in a robbery and served time in a Kentucky prison)

J

James, Frank (Died in Kearney, Missouri, 1915)
James, Jesse Woodson (Shot to death by Robert Ford in St. Joseph, Missouri, April 3, 1882)
James, William
Jarrette, John (Later became owner of a large sheep ranch in Arizona)

Jobson, Smith
Jones, Jim
Jones, Payne (Killed by Jim Crow Chiles)

K

Kelly, James
Kelly, Tom
Kennedy, Dave
Kennedy, Steve
Kennedy, Sterling
Kerr, Christian name unknown
Ketchum, Al
Key, Foster
King, Willis
Kinney, Dick
Knight, Christian name unknown
Koger, Ed
Koger, John W.

L

Lea, Joe (Died in Roswell, New Mexico, in 1904)
Letten, Ling
Lilly, James (Went to Kentucky with Quantrill)
Little, James (Went to Kentucky with Quantrill)
Little John
Little, Thomas (Hanged by a mob at Warrensburg, Missouri)
Long, Peyton (Went to Kentucky with Quantrill)
Lotspeach, William
Luckett, Christian name unknown

M

Maddox, George
Maddox, Morgan T.
Maddox, Richard (Killed by a Cherokee Indian after the war)
Marshall, Ed
Marshall, James
Maupin, John
Maupin, Thomas (Became a Texas cattleman after the war)
Maxwell, Ambrose
Maxwell, Thomas
Miller, Edward (Killed by Jesse James after the war)

Miller, McClelland (Clell) (Killed at Northfield Bank raid, 1876)
Monkers, "Red"
Moody, Jasper
Morrow, Benjamin J.
Morris, James
Murray, "Plunk"

Mc
McAnich, Henry
McArtor, James T.
McCabe, James
McCorkle, John
McCorkle, Joseph
McCorkle, Josiah
McCorkle, Thomas
McCoy, Arthur
McCoy, Richard
McDowell, John
McGuire, Andy (Hanged, June 1867)
McGuire, Bill
McIlvaine, John
McIvor, John
McMurtry, Lee

N
Nicholson, Arch
Nicholson, Joseph
Noland, Edward (Went to Kentucky with Quantrill)
Noland, Henry (Went to Kentucky with Quantrill)
Noland, William (Went to Kentucky with Quantrill)
Norfolk, John

O
O'Donald, Patrick
Owens, Thomas

P
Palmer, Chris (Went to Kentucky with Quantrill)
Parmer, Allen H. (Died at Wichita Falls, Texas, in 1927. He was Jesse James' brother-in-law)
Parr, "Buster"

Parvin, Hence
Parvin, Lafe
Patterson, Hank
Pence, "Bud" (Went to Kentucky with Quantrill)
Pence, "Donney" (Went to Kentucky with Quantrill)
Perkins, Christian name unknown
Perry, Joab (Deserted Quantrill after the Lawrence raid)
Peyton, Christian name unknown
Pool, Dave (Settled at Sherman, Texas, after the war)
Pool, John
Pope, Sam
Porter, Henry (Went to Kentucky with Quantrill)
Pringle, John

R

Railly, Lon
Ralston, Crockett
Read, James (Killed in Texas in 1874)
Renick, Clarke (Ordered Riley Crawford executed)
Reynolds, William
Robertson, Gooley
Robinson, George
Robinson, William (Hanged in Kentucky in 1865)
Roder, William
Rollen, Christian name unknown
Rollen (second), Christian name unknown
Ross, John (Went to Kentucky with Quantrill)
Rudd, John
Rupe, John
Ryan, Volney

S

Sanders, Tid
Schull, Bonn
Scott, Albert
Scott, Fernando
Shepherd, Frank
Shepherd, George (Spent time in Kentucky Penitentiary)
Shepherd, Oliver (Killed by police officers in 1868)
Shores, Stephen

ROSTER OF GUERRILLAS

Simmons, Christian name unknown
Skaggs, Larkin Milton (Killed in Lawrence, Kansas)
Smith, William
Southwick, A. B.
Southwick, C. H.
Stewart, Charles
Stewart, William
Story, "Bud"
Stuart, William H.
Sturgeon, Christian name unknown
Sutherland, Jack
Sutherland, Zeke

T

Talley, George
Tarkington, William
Tate, David
Taylor, Charles Fletcher (Later a member of the Missouri legislature)
Thrailkill, John (Captain in Quantrill's band)
Tigue, Nat
Todd, George (Killed at Independence, Missouri, in 1864)
Todd, Thomas
Toler, Christian name unknown
Toley, J. B.
Tolliver, Anse
Toothum, Christian name unknown
Traber, Thomas
Traber, Zach
Trow, Harrison B. (Identified body of Jesse James)
Tucker, James
Tucker, Morris J.
Tucker, William

V

Van Meter, John
Vaughn, Dan
Vaughn, James A. (Wrote a book after the war; claimed he was Frank James)
Vaughn, Joseph

Venable, Randall M. (Went to Kentucky with Quantrill)

W
Wade, Sam
Walker, Andrew Y.
Warren, John
Wayman, F. Luther
Webb, Charley
Webster, Noah
Welch, Warren
Wells, Polk
West, Richard
White, James
White, John
Whitsett, James Simeon
Wigginton, George
Williams, Hank
William, James
Wilson, Dave
Wood, Bennett
Wood, Robert
Wood, Christian name unknown
Wyatt, Cave

Y
Yeager, Richard
Young, Joseph
Younger, Chris
Younger, James (Committed suicide in 1902 in Minnesota)
Younger, John (Killed by officers at Osceola, Missouri, in 1874)
Younger, Thomas Coleman (Cole) (Died at Lee's Summit, Missouri, in 1916)

This completes the authentic list of the 296 men who rode with the famous William Clarke Quantrill at one time or another. Of course they were not always all together. Only during the Lawrence raid did Quantrill's entire command act as a unit. Even then certain new recruits such as Jesse James were not included. Besides, many who had previously ridden with him were not present on that day.